HERMAN CHARLES BOSMAN

COLD STONE JUG

Herman Charles Bosman
COLD STONE JUG

HUMAN & ROUSSEAU

CAPE TOWN · PRETORIA

FIRST PRINTING 1969
SECOND PRINTING 1971
THIRD PRINTING 1975

ISBN 0 7981 0573 9

NEW EDITION FIRST PUBLISHED IN 1969 BY
HUMAN & ROUSSEAU PUBLISHERS (PTY.) LTD.,
3–9 ROSE STREET, CAPE TOWN; 239 PRETORIUS STREET, PRETORIA
PRINTED BY PRINTPAK (CAPE) LTD., DACRES AVENUE, EPPING

Dedicated to Helena, my wife

A CHRONICLE:
BEING THE UNIMPASSIONED
RECORD OF A SOMEWHAT LENGTHY
SOJOURN IN PRISON

Preamble

"Murder," I answered.

There were about a dozen prisoners in the cells at Marshall Square. It was getting on towards the late afternoon of a Sunday that we had spent locked up in a cell that was three-quarters underground and that had barred apertures opening on to the pavement at the corner of McLaren and Marshall Streets, Johannesburg. I had been arrested about fifteen or sixteen hours before.

Those first hours in the cells at Marshall Square, serving as the overture to a long period of imprisonment in the Swartklei Great Prison, were the most miserable I have ever known. By standing on a bench you could get near enough to the barred opening to catch an occasional glimpse of the underneath part of the shoe-leather of passing pedestrians, who, on that dreary Sunday afternoon, consisted almost entirely of natives. The motley collection of prisoners inside the cell took turns in getting on to the bench and trying to attract the attention of the passers-by. Now and again a native would stop. A lengthy discussion would follow. Occasionally, (this constituting a triumphant termination to the interview) a piece of lighted cigarette-end would be dropped in through that little hole in the wall against the pavement. This was over twenty years ago. But it is still like that. You can go and look there.

For the rest of the time the dozen inmates of the cell carried on a desultory conversation, a lot of it having to do with what appeared to be highly unbecoming activities on the part of plain-clothes members of the police force, who seemed to spend all their waking hours in working up spurious cases against law-abiding citizens. Then, when it was getting towards late afternoon, one of the prisoners, a dapper little fellow who had done most of the talking and who seemed to exercise some sort of leadership in the cell, felt that it was time we all got sort of cosy together, and started taking more of a personal interest in one another's affairs.

"I'm in for liquor-selling, myself," he announced to a man standing next to him, "What they pinch you for?"

"Stealing a wheel-barrow from the p.w.d.," was the reply, "Not that I done it, mind you. But that's the charge."

"And what are you in for?" the cell-boss demanded of the next man.

"Drunk and disorderly and indecent exposure," came the answer.

"And what's your charge?"

"Forgery. And if I drop this time I'll get seven years."

And so this dapper little fellow who was doing the questioning worked his way through the whole lot until it came to my turn.

"Say, what are you pinched for?" he asked, eyeing me narrowly.

"Murder," I said. And in my tone there was no discourtesy. And I did not glower much. I only added, "And I'm not feeling too good."

"Struth!" my interrogator remarked. And his jaw dropped. And that bunch of prisoners in the cell, the whole dozen of them, moved right across to the other side, to the corner that was furthest away from me.

Chapter 1

IT WAS A SUNDAY on which the Dutch Reformed Church was honouring the mothers of the country.

And for the mother's day service in the Swartklei Prison chapel the Predikant had brought along a large number of paper labels, coloured respectively green and purple. The labels were passed round. This was something new and exciting. It made all us convicts attending the Dutch Reformed service in the prison chapel feel important people, somehow. If your mother was still alive you were expected to fix a green strip of paper on to the lapel of your brown corduroy jacket. If your mother was dead you fastened on a purple strip. No pins were provided, but the backs of these strips of coloured paper were gummed. So we stuck the labels on with spit. And we sat there, on the wooden benches, straight up and very proud, feeling not only that we were doing homage to our mothers, but that we were participating in a ceremony that was on that day being observed in the magical world known as "outside".

"They are having mothers' day outside, also," one convict would say to another.

People in churches outside, men as well as women (the entrancing sound of the word "women"!) were wearing little labels like these on their breasts. We were just like *outside* for those minutes during which the service in the prison chapel lasted. And we relished that period to the full, basking in the pride of being, for a while, like people who were free to roam the streets. Able to do the same things that men and women who were not in prison were doing.

Sharing in *their* emotions. Feeling about things the way *they* felt.

The Predikant spoke in a very moving way about our mothers, and about us, also, about those of us whose mothers were still alive and who accordingly were privileged to wear green labels, and about those of us who had unfortunately lost our mothers, and so wore purple labels in sorrowful remembrance. (The Predikant pointedly made no reference to those convicts in his congregation who, through ignorance or misguided zeal, had stuck whole rows of labels, purple and green mixed up just anyhow, on to their jackets, like they were military ribbons). The result was, what with the hymn-singing and all, that the convicts got worked up to such a pitch of emotionalism that even the most hardened blue-coats (habitual criminals) broke down and sobbed. Men who had spent many years in prison and had grown grey behind bars, looking at the pathetic strips of coloured paper stuck on to their lapels with spit, dissolved into tears.

When the service ended and we tramped down the iron stairs back to the cells, (encountering the Methodists, who were coming up the stairs as we were going down) a blue-coat in front of me, his face still tearful after the sermon, inadvertently collided with a convict tramping up to attend the Methodist service.

"As jy my weer stamp sal ek jou donder," the blue-coat said, but his tone was kindly. The thought of the way he had been breaking his mother's heart through the years had softened him. His language, through long habit, held low menace. But his tone was unexpectedly mild.

As the law used to be (and still is, I believe), after a man has committed the same offence a number of times – twice, I think, in some cases, and about twenty-seven times in others – the judge in passing sentence warns the culprit that if he again appears before a court of law and is convicted he will be declared an habitual criminal. That means that the word "Indeterminate sentence" gets inscribed on his ticket. His release from prison is then a matter that rests with the Board of Visitors, who come to the Swartklei Great Prison to interview him once a year. Sometimes the Board recommends him for discharge after he has served six years. Usually the period is seven, eight, nine years and longer. But when he is eventually discharged from prison this man is placed on a five years' period of probation. He is not allowed to consort with fellow ex-convicts (what other friends has he got, incidentally, in the outside world that has forgotten him during those long years behind bars?) He is not allowed to frequent pubs. And if at any time during the five years of probation he gets convicted on the most minor offence, something for which he could get a five pound fine or a few days' imprisonment, he goes back to prison to serve the indeterminate sentence all over again.

As they say in prison, he goes back to do his second blue-coat. This time he serves a longer stretch than for the first indeterminate sentence. When he comes out the second time, it is the same thing over again. The five years' ticket-of-leave. I believe there are some men in the Swartklei Great Prison to-day busy with their fourth blue-coat. It is possible, through the indeterminate sentence system, for a man to spend thirty years and more in prison, with intervals of only a few weeks or a few months or a few days at a time, and all through his having committed a number of minor offences while out on ticket. It is possible, of course, to spend as long as forty or fifty years behind bars in this way – that is, if you live that long.

The ordinary convict wears a brown corduroy jacket, rather ill-fitting and shapeless, and knee-breeches and long woollen stockings, black with red stripes, and a peculiar kind of footwear, halfway between a shoe and a boot. But instead of the brown corduroy jacket the indeterminate sentence convict wears a blue serge jacket, as a distinctive garb. Hence the term "blue-coat." At exercise in the yards, in the workshops, in the cell corridors, everywhere, except in the first offenders' section, the sprinkling of prisoners wearing blue jacketsis a characteristic feature of life in the Swartklei Great Prison. I noticed that, with each year that passed, the percentage of convicts wearing blue jackets got higher. The imposition of the indeterminate sentence did not seem to act as a deterrent to recidivism. Oh, yes, I almost forgot – on the breast-pocket of the blue-coat the letters "I.S." are sewn on in red. The letters stand, of course, for "Indeterminate Sentence", but in terms of prison irony the letters "I.S." have long ago been interpreted as signifying "I'm Settled."

In prison the blue-coat occupies a position of some degree of importance. He doesn't rank as high as a head-warder, maybe. But his social standing is certainly a considerable cut above that of a warder-recruit. A blue-coat is even higher than a murderer. One's prestige inside the prison is in direct proportion to the length of the sentence one is serving and is also based on the number of times one has been convicted. Thus, a first offender who is doing a life sentence, while he rates pretty high as a prison "head", hasn't got quite the same status as a lifer with a number of previous convictions. The more time you do, the better you are supposed to know the ropes. And nothing is more annoying to the genuine long-timer, somebody engaged on a stretch of from ten to twenty years, or life, than to find an inferior person, sentenced to a trivial matter of two or three years only, giving himself the airs of a "head," and speaking out of his turn generally.

And so the blue-coat goes on doing his time, year in and year out. Seven years, eight years, nine years. And then out for a short while on ticket, finding himself in a world that has changed utterly; alone and friendless, certain of one thing only, and that is that before the five years of probation are up doom will have descended on him again in the form of a conviction, for a serious or a trivial offence, it doesn't matter which, and he will have to start on the indeterminate sentence all over again And how the world changes while you are doing a stretch. When you come out you find that the places you used to know in Johannesburg have vanished. Sky-scrapers have gone up where there were tin shanties. And people's habits. They are altogether different. Whether the people have changed their ways, or whether it is you who have altered, having grown so inured to the prison methods of doing things – this is something that you just don't know, and that you don't care about, either.

But when I walk about the streets, and I see the crowds of men and women, with all the multitude of expressions on their faces, and all the different sorts of light in their eyes; and I feel the warm glow of human beings, and my nostrils are filled with the heady stink of human beings, and something inside me comes alive to the joy and pathos of humanity – then I sometimes think, for a few fleeting moments, of the blue-coats in the Swartklei Great Prison. I think of the long prison years in front of them and behind them. I see them hemmed in by brown walls and brown years. I think of these men leading their silent lives. And I hope that God will go with them, through all those years.

3

Now for the murderers. Compared with the blue-coats, they are rather a jolly lot. The majority of them are first offenders. That is not surprising, of course. Murder being the crime it is, it is unlikely that anybody will feel like committing it a number of times. For that matter, you're not allowed to commit murder a number of times ... The result is that by far the majority of murderers doing stretches in the Swartklei Great Prison are first offenders. A murderer never comes back to prison, either. It is almost as though murder, the capital crime, is the only one that appeals to him. The other offences under common law seem too tame, by comparison, to be able to tempt him. The murderer is a strange figure; not pathetic, like the blue-coat; but lonely somehow; almost like the eagle. But also with the lost bewilderment of a child.

In prison, the murderer, unlike the blue-coat, does not wear a distinctive garb. He is not dressed by the authorities in a way to single him out from the other convicts – bank-robbers, forgers, illicit gold-buyers, rapists and the rest. There is no need for men to put any distinguishing marks on a murderer's clothes. Cain's mark is there for all to read. Murder is a doomed sign to wear on your brow.

4

Disguise it how one will, the fact is that the Swartklei Great Prison is dominated, spiritually as well as architecturally, by the gallows chamber, whose doors rise up, massive and forbidding, at the end of the main wing in the building – the penal corridors.

The hangings are the worst part of life inside the prison. When a man has been condemned to death on the Rand or in any other Transvaal centre he is brought over to the Swartklei

14

Great Prison, where he is lodged in the condemned cell adjacent to the gallows until such time as he is either reprieved or hanged. The period of waiting in that cell next to the gallows varies from about five weeks to two months. Then the case is settled one way or the other. Either the sheriff arrives with a printed document bearing the title "Greetings" in heavy black scroll and he notifies the condemned man that his execution has been set down for the morning after the next, or the Governor of the prison walks in, accompanied by the chief warder, and he informs the prisoner that the Governor-General has decided to commute his sentence to one of imprisonment, the term varying usually from ten years to life.

But during all this time the shadow of this hanging lies like a pall over the inmates of the prison, warders as well as convicts. During most of the months of the year the condemned cells are empty. There is nobody waiting up there at the end of the penal section with the death sentence suspended over him. But when the condemned cells are occupied, things in the prison are rotten all round. There is something inside the most hardened warder or anti-social convict that makes him shudder at the thought of death, of violent death, of the gruesome ceremony of doing a man to death above a dark hole, at a set time, with legal formality that does not extend beyond handcuffs and leg-irons and a sack drawn over the condemned man's head and a piece of coarse rope knotted behind his ear.

On the morning of a hanging the cells are unlocked half-an-hour later than usual. The prisoners arrive at their workshops half-an-hour late. The cells are all locked at the hour of the hanging and the morning bell doesn't ring until the execution is over. The man in the condemned cell must not be allowed to know how near his hour has actually come. They say it is all done very efficiently. They say that it takes less than two minutes from the moment the hangman has unlocked the door of the condemned cell until he has got the prisoner trussed and pinioned and with the rope round his neck, waiting for the trap-door to fall. When the trap drops it is with a reverberation that shakes the whole prison building, and the bell rings, and the cells are unlocked and the convicts march out to work.

I dislike according so much space to the details of the hangings, but these things loom like a shadow over the prison all the time, like an unpleasant odour, and they make life inside the prison a lot gloomier than it would otherwise be. The six hundred convicts and the hundred warders in the prison share to some extent the feelings of the man who is being dropped through the trap-door, and the fountain-head of life grows discoloured. I don't suppose very much can be done about it. After all, prison isn't supposed to be a place where you can just spend a few happy, carefree years at will.

*

I remember that I had company in the condemned cell. There was another man there, also under sentence of death, when I arrived. We were separated from each other by two rows of bars and wire netting, which formed a little passage in which the warder on duty paced up and down. The warders watched us night and day, working in four-hour shifts, with the lights on all the time. That other man's name was Stoffels. We were provided with cigarettes, which the warder would light for us through the wire-netting. I remember the smell of disinfectant in that cell. It is a kind of disinfectant that they use in a number of Government institutions. The smell is strong but not unpleasant. Only the other day I got a whiff of this same disinfectant in a post-office corridor. And in one punch that odour brought the past back to me like it was now. I even looked round to see whether the sanitary pail was still there, in the corner.

But I can recall only the external impressions, the surface things, which I have learnt are not realities at all.

I can remember the jokes Stoffels and I made, talking to each other through two sets of steel netting and bars, with the warder in between. And the questions we asked the warders about life inside the prison. We had to ask these questions of the warders, we two, who were in the prison but not of it. And the stories the warders had to relate to us, in the long nights when we couldn't get to sleep, made life as a convict inside a prison seem very alluring – just simply because it was life. And when we heard the convicts march out to work in the mornings, their footsteps heavy on the concrete floor of the hall far removed from us, their passage sounded like the tread of kings. And when a warder mentioned to us the fact that he had that morning had occasion, in the course of an altercation, to hit a convict over the head with his baton, I know how I felt about that convict, how I envied him, how infinitely privileged I felt he was to be able to be regarded by a warder as a live person, as somebody that could be hit over the head. For no warder would dream of hitting a condemned man with a baton. To a warder a condemned man was something already dead.

Because we had been sentenced to be hanged, Stoffels and I were accorded certain privileges. For one thing, we didn't have to get our hair cropped short, like the other convicts, with a pair of number nought clippers. And when I was taken out on exercise, into the prison yard, twice a day, and I saw other convicts from a distance, and I saw how short their hair was, and I felt my own hair, long and wavy, and I understood what my long hair signified – then I didn't feel too good. I even hoped that, somehow, by mistake, somebody would come in and say that the chief warder had ordered my hair to be cut short. Just so I wouldn't have to flaunt, in the exercise yard, that awful thing that made me different from the hard-labour convicts. Long hair and the rope. . . . A short rope.

Of course, Stoffels and I affected unconcern, there in the condemned cell. We spent much of our waking hours in pulling the warders' legs. We didn't know, then, that we were in actual fact engaged in a time-honoured prison pastime. We didn't know that "kidding" to warders was a sport regularly indulged in by prison lags, and that this form of recreation had venerable traditions. We didn't know all that. We merely followed our natural bent of trying to be funny, and we found, afterwards, that we were all the time conforming to accepted prison custom. It must be that prison was, after all, the right place for Stoffels and me. Because to this aspect of it, at all events, to the part of it connected with pulling a warder's leg, we took like ducks to water.

There was one warder whom Stoffels and I nicknamed the Clown. He had not been in the prison service very long and had only recently been transferred to the Swartklei Great Prison from a native gaol in Barberton. We joshed him unmercifully. He was a young fellow in his early twenties, but Stoffels and I addressed him as though he were a man of the world with infinitely wide experience and an oracle of learning. He afforded us many nights of first-class entertainment, during the dreary hours between ten at night and two in the morning, when we could not sleep and were afraid to trust our heads to the hard pallet, in case when we woke up in the morning it would be to find the sheriff standing at the door, with the death-warrant.

The Clown had a very simple heart. One night, through a

process of not very subtle flattery, we got him to acknowledge that he could dance rather well. We also got him to admit that, in general, men were envious of his ball-room accomplishments, and that, behind his back, they said many nasty things about him, such as that he danced like a sick hippopotamus, or the way a duck waddles. All because they were jealous of him. We even got him so far as to show us a few of the latest dance-steps. For this purpose he took off his heavy warder's boots. At the Clown's demonstration, in his stockinged feet, of the then-fashionable black-bottom, Stoffels and I laughed uproariously. We explained to him, of course, that we were laughing at the thought that jealous males could have come to such ludicrously erroneous conclusions about his dancing, merely because they viewed everything he did through the green gaze of envy. Thereupon the Clown joined in the laughter, thus making Stoffels and me roar louder than ever.

"Didn't they perhaps, in their jealousy, even say –" I started off again, when we all suddenly stopped laughing. For a key grated in the outer door and the night head-warder entered.

"What's all this?" he demanded, "The convicts the other end of the hall are complaining they can't sleep, the way you men in the condemned cell keep on laughing all night. And this isn't the first night, neither."

The night head-warder looked at us sternly. There seemed something gravely irregular in a situation in which two condemned men were keeping a whole prison establishment awake with indecorous laughter.

"You condemned men mustn't laugh so loud," he said, "The hard labour convicts got to sleep. They got to work all day. You two don't do nothing but smoke cigarettes all day long and crack jokes. You'll get yourselves in serious trouble if the Governor finds out you keep the whole prison awake night after night, romping about and laughing in the condemned cells."

I wondered, vaguely, what more serious trouble we could get into than we were already in. But at that moment the night head-warder happened to look down at the Clown's feet. So it was his turn to laugh. The Clown certainly cut a ridiculous figure, with shapeless pieces of feet leaking out of his socks.

"Where's your boots?" the night head-warder demanded, his tone midway between a threat and a guffaw, "Don't you know as you can't come on duty improperly dressed? What sort of an example do you think you are to these two condemned men? And look at all them pertaters in your socks. I never seen so many pertaters in a sock. More pertater than sock. With all them pertaters you ought to be working in the kitchen. Come on, now. Quick about it. Put on the other boot, too. What you want to take them off for, anyway? To show these condemned men your pertaters, I suppose. Or maybe you got bunions. Yes, must be bunions. I suppose you got bunions on your feet through walking about the streets looking for trollops."

With that sally, and still guffawing, the night head-warder departed. There certainly seemed to be something in the atmosphere of the cell adjacent to the gallows that was provocative of a spirit of clean fun. The condemned cell air seemed to be infectiously mirth-making.

"Now, isn't that just what we have been saying?" Stoffels asked of the Clown when the three of us were alone together, once more, "How do you like that for jealousy? The moment the night head-warder sees you he starts picking you out. What do you think of that? And so ridiculous, too. How can he say you got those bunions on your feet –"

"But I haven't got bunions," the Clown asserted, "You

know as well as I do that I took off my boots to show you my –"

"Those terrible bunions," Stoffels persisted, ignoring the Clown's remonstrances, "How can he say you got those corns and bunions *and blisters* walking after whores in the street? Has he ever seen you walking after a whore in the street? Come on, answer me, has he ever seen you?"

"I don't know what he's seen or what he hasn't seen," the Clown answered, "I only know that the only times I've ever walked about looking for a whore it was in the other end of the town from where he stays. It was –"

6

Warders all say that the job in a prison they like least is that of guarding a condemned man. They say it makes them too melancholy. I think I can understand why. If I was a warder I would also get a bellyful of this sort of nonsense. Gallows half-laughs.

There was one warder who gave Stoffels and me a bit of trouble at the start. I don't mean that he bothered us in any way, or that he was offensive. The trouble was simply that we couldn't get him to talk. No matter how cunningly we baited our traps, he would never fall. He was too wise. His name was Van Graan, and he had been in the prison service for a good many years. We tried him with practically everything. He would have none of it. We tried him on that hardy annual, promotion. We also held out the bait of a discussion on long leave. (We had found that this was also a sore point with the warders. According to what they told us, the granting of long leave was intimately bound up with nepotism. Only the Governor's favourites got granted it.)

One evening we again tried Van Graan out on promotion.

"I suppose you have been in the prison service a very long time?" I essayed, "Funny how one can always tell the difference between an old hand and a new recruit. I can't imagine you ever having been a recruit, meneer. The way you know the ropes. Anybody can see it on you. Nobody would ever try any stunts on you."

"But I also made mistakes at the start," Warder van Graan acknowledged, "I also had to learn. But perhaps it come a bit easier to me than to most –"

"Brains," Stoffels vociferated, "Brains. What I say is if a man has got brains you can't keep him down. Unless it's jealousy. Look at you, now, meneer. Look what brains you got. And look how many years you been in the service. And what's your reward? You're not even a head-warder."

"I'd sooner be just a ordinary warder, like what I am," Warder van Graan answered, turning nasty, "Than be in your boots."

So that attempt had also gone awry. But we got Warder van Graan in the end. We could never have believed that he would have succumbed to so obvious a snare.

"Why I wouldn't like to be a warder," Stoffels announced one evening in a tone the very casual and disarming quality of which should have put Warder van Graan on his guard, "is because of all the backbiting that goes on in a prison. Now, that is where I would be different if I was a warder. I wouldn't go and talk about other warders, behind their backs, to convicts. I would have too much self-respect."

"Some people got no self-respect at all," Warder van Graan nodded his agreement, "And what does one man want to go and scandal behind another man's back? Does he think he'll get more pay for it?"

"And to convicts, too," I interposed, "I mean if a warder has fallen so low that he talks to other convicts about a fellow-warder, what won't he go and say about this same warder to the chief, or even to the Governor? A warder that's so low as to gossip with convicts will fall so low, after a while, as to talk to the Governor also –"

"Perhaps he has already fallen so low," Warder van Graan exclaimed, "But who is this warder you are talking about?"

He was a goner then, of course. Poor old Warder van Graan.

"No, no," Stoffels replied, "It's nothing at all, meneer. I was only thinking that I wouldn't like to be a warder, here in the Swartklei Great Prison, if you understand what I mean. I wouldn't like to think that day after day I do my duty honestly, the best I can, and then all the time there is that other warder going behind my back and saying things about me that –"

"Oh, so it's him, is it?" Warder van Graan demanded. "That bastard Snake-Eye. I could have knowed Snake-Eye was up to no good. And him a elder in the church and all. And I know what he says about me, also. He says I lumbers."

"Lumbers?" I repeated. It sounded like halitosis.

"He says I smuggles in tobacco and things," Warder van Graan explained, "Now, I been suspecting that about him a long time, that he goes about saying as I lumbers."

"Whereas, of course, he is the one that lumbers," I replied, very brightly, "It is only when you are yourself guilty of a thing that you accuse others."

"What I knows about him," Warder van Graan said, and he lowered his voice and spoke very slowly and solemnly, "If I was to say what I knows about Snake-Eye, he'd be sitting here where you are."

I affected a start.

23

"Not as bad as that, surely, meneer?" I exclaimed, "You don't mean to say that what you know about him can get him hanged. Who did he murder? I always felt there was something about that Snake-Eye –"

"No, no, not murder," Warder van Graan exclaimed, "Not as bad as the condemned cell. What I mean to say is he'd be in prison if I was to tell all I know. He made over fifty pounds the month before last, lumbering in tobacco to convicts whose people have got the money. He lumbers it in hidden under his rain-cape. What would he say if I asked the Governor why does Snake-Eye wear a rain-cape when it is a clear, hot night in the middle of the summer, and not a cloud in the sky?"

"But, of course, you would never do a thing like that," I responded, "We all know you got principle."

"And what about that refrigerator that was sent for repairs to the fitters-shop from the reserve?" Warder van Graan demanded, "Through whose backyard did eight convicts carry that refrigerator one Tuesday morning. I ask you. Through whose?"

"Surely not –" I began hesitantly, "Surely not through –"

"Yus," Warder van Graan said, "Through none other's backyard. I seen it with my own eyes."

Warder van Graan was caught. He was porridge in our hands, after that. If Stoffels or I would have wanted brandy or dagga smuggled into the condemned cell for us, Warder van Graan would have lumbered it in.

I should like to include just this final story about the Clown.

I have explained that the warder walks up and down that little passage between the two condemned cells. The warder is also locked in. They do that so as to keep a condemned man doubly secure: first, locked inside his own cell, and, secondly, locked in with the warder in a larger cell, comprising the two condemned cells and the warder's passage. But the warder is all right, there. He's got a revolver. Only, he can't get out during the four hours of his shift. The section-warder has to come and unlock him. But he's got a bell-button that he can push whenever there's trouble. Each warder, when he enters the cell, is provided with a tin vessel, cylindrical and about a foot high – like a native's dinner-pail, but taller – containing drinking-water. When the Clown came on duty, at ten p.m., it was customary because of the lateness of the hour, to put two tins of water into the warder's passage, one for the Clown and one for the warder who came on duty after him. That meant that the cleaner in the section did not have to be awakened at two o'clock in the morning to get the next warder a tin of drinking-water.

But because the Clown had been transferred to Swartklei from Barberton only recently, he was not conversant with all the niceties of condemned cell routine. Consequently, he thought that both tins were for his own use. He would drink water out of one tin, whenever he got thirsty, and regularly, about ten minutes before the next warder (whom we nicknamed Jannie) came in to relieve him, the Clown would wash his hands in the other tin of drinking-water. He used my soap and towel, or Stoffels's soap and towel, whichever was nearer to hand. (Unfortunately, I find that I must again interrupt with a parenthesis. But that is the prison's fault, not mine. I can't help it that prison routine should be so absurdly complicated. Anyway, each time, last thing at night, after Stoffels and I had had our supper, the section-warder would order us to put our empty enamel dixies outside – and also our pieces of soap and our towels. This measure was probably incorporated into the regulations in order to prevent condemned criminals from suffocating themselves with the towels, or from making themselves unnecessarily ill through eating pieces of prison-soap).

Anyway, two pieces of soap and two towels – mine and Stoffels's respectively – would be lying in the corner of his passage when the Clown came in, and there would also be two tins of water. As I have said, the Clown would regularly drink up the water in one tin, and wash his hands in the other.

Most nights, Jannie, the warder who relieved the Clown, would stay on duty right through until six o'clock, without getting thirsty. But those nights when he wanted a drink of water and he picked up the tin that the Clown had washed his hands in, Jannie would curse the whole prison up and down. Prison-warders as a class are not distinguished in respect of being particularly clean-mouthed. And Jannie seemed to be much more fastidious about what went into his mouth than he was about what came out. In fact, what came out of his mouth each time he tasted that water in which the Clown had performed his ablutions, were words and expressions that I felt no soap in the world would ever wash clean again.

"—— the cleaners," Jannie would splutter, "The —— water tastes —— soapy again. The lazy bastards of —— of —— cleaners are too —— lazy to wash the —— blasted soap off from the inside of the —— tin when they put in water for me."

This went on for about a week. Some nights Jannie went off duty without having a drink of water. That was all right. But whenever he drank the Clown's soapy water he would get into a rage that had him cursing for the better part of the night. Stoffels and I never thought of enlightening Jannie about the true state of affairs, preferring to let him blame it on the cleaners. Similarly, we did not think it worthwhile to inform the Clown that every time he washed his hands it was in another man's drinking-water. The situation seemed pregnant with possibilities that we didn't want spoilt.

Then, one night, it happened. It was past one o'clock. The Clown was somewhat circumspect about ringing the bell for the section-warder in a matter of that nature . . .

Stoffels and I said no word to each other about what we had witnessed. We went to lie down under our blankets, and lay hoping for the best. The Clown went off duty, Jannie coming in to relieve him. Nothing had been noticed. Could it really be possible that so unique a piece of enjoyment could come the way of two sorry felons such as Stoffels and I? Surely, it was too much to hope for . . . Could two men, condemned to death, resting for a brief while at the foot of the gallows, be placed in the way of so rare a thrill? The genius that watches over criminals was with Stoffels and me that night. In the early hours of the morning, when I could hardly stand the tension any longer, Jannie got thirsty. I heard the bottom of the tin grate against the concrete of the floor. I heard Jannie draw in his breath before drinking. Then, oh, rich and ineffable and unforgettable ecstasy, oh, memorable delight, I heard – glug, glug, just like that – I heard Jannie drink. And he went on drinking. Eventually, he sighed, deeply, and I heard him put down the tin.

"Yes, I am thirsty, to-night," Jannie muttered, half to himself. I couldn't stand it any longer.

"Meneer," I said, "The tin. The tin you drink out of. There was no soap in it to-night, was there?"

"No," Jannie answered, "But it tasted funny, all the same."

"Like – like what did it taste, meneer?" I enquired, struggling hard to keep my voice level.

"Well, if I didn't know better," Jannie said, "If I didn't

know that it was quite impossible, I would say that it tasted a lot like ——."

So Stoffels and I both jumped up from our blankets and informed Jannie that it was.

Chapter 2

I

WE KEPT ON indulging in spasmodic frivolities and pulling the warders' legs right until the end. But, of course, it wasn't the same any more when I was left alone in the condemned cell after Stoffels got hanged. Still, I did my best. And there were several nights, when I was there, alone with the warder, on which the night head-warder had to come round and request me to laugh and talk in more subdued tones. I was giving the condemned cell a bad name, he said. But I admit frankly that it wasn't the same, any more, after Stoffels was no longer there.

I am afraid that the reader will have got rather a nebulous sort of impression of this man Stoffels. I am afraid he won't appear to the reader as a creature of flesh and blood. And that is only because I was never able to feel about Stoffels either, that he was a man in a world of men. Perhaps it was because he was going to be hanged, and although he himself naturally entertained hopes of a reprieve, hoping against hope all the time, there was something inside him, his inner life force, that knew otherwise. At all events, I only realised, after Stoffels had been hanged, how much I missed him, and how little I knew about him, really.

When I entered the condemned cell he was already there. He had got there a few weeks before me. And I was with him for about a month. During all this time I made no real human contact with him. It must have been that the thing inside him knew that he was doomed to die, with the result that he gave out no more human warmths or light or shadow.

As my companion in the death-cell for more than four weeks, Stoffels had done a good deal to cheer me up. And yet, on the morning of his execution, there was nothing I could think of saying to him. I could think of no last quip to make. I could think of no final word of comfort. In the shadow of the gallows, I had found, a jest or a solemn speech meant just about the same thing. But even if I could have thought up something to say, I would have had no opportunity of saying it. For early that morning two warders came and fetched me out of my own cell and locked me in a cell two doors away. They didn't lock the door, though, but only the grille gate. And from the sounds I heard later on, when the hangman came to perform his office, it sounded as though everything went off very efficiently. There was the tramping of feet on the iron stairs and the sound of doors being locked and unlocked, and no sound of voices. No orders had to be given. Each man knew what was expected of him, even Stoffels, – who played his part tolerably well, considering the fact that he was not rehearsed in it and was getting no pay for it.

The rest of the actors in this early morning drama of the gallows – the Governor, the warders, the doctor, the hangman, the chaplain – were all salaried officials of the administration. Only Stoffels was giving his services free.

I heard what sounded like a quick scuffle, then many footfalls. And then a muffled noise in which I recognised Stoffels's voice, but with difficulty, for only part of that noise seemed to come out of his throat. The rest of it seemed to have come out of his belly. More heavy footfalls and doors creaking on hinges. And still no rapped out words of command. Then a mighty slam that shook the whole building, rattling the pannikin on the floor of the cell in which I was. And it was all over. I looked at the warder guarding me on the other side of the grille. His face was a greenish-white. Then the bell rang. And there were voices, and the sound of much movement, and the noise and commotion of a prison with six hundred convicts beginning the day's routine. I was not as badly shaken by this experience as I thought I would have been. Perhaps it was because, as I have indicated, I had not felt in Stoffels's veins and lungs the blood and breath of life any more during the period of our having known each other.

2

I don't want to waste any more time writing about the condemned cell. I want to get on with the next part of this story. In fact, I want to get out of the condemned cell as quick as possible. As quick as I got out of it that afternoon when the Governor came up and informed me that I had been reprieved. I was asleep on my blankets on the floor, that afternoon. I was dreaming, but I forget what about. And I awoke to find the Governor and the chief warder and the section officer and the warder on duty in the death cell, all together standing in a ring around me. I woke up and rubbed my eyes. The Governor was talking. And on a sudden the import of his words and his visit dawned on me. It was the Governor who had called on me, and not the sheriff. Not the sheriff. Then I got the gist of it. The Governor was saying that my sentence had been commuted to a term of imprisonment with hard labour for so many years. I got out of that condemned cell in such a hurry that I didn't hear all of the years. And afterwards when I did find out (because they took me down into the hall later on and got the number of years written on my ticket) that knowledge did not sober me up.

On the way down to the hall the head-warder addressed me in terms of stern admonition.

"You're a bleeding hard-labour —— convict now," he said, "See? And we don't want none of your —— sanguinary cheek here. You broke your —— mother's heart and we'll break your —— heart. We tame lions here. First peep out of you, my man, and I'll see you get six day's solitary on spare diet. Pick up your step, there! You're not a blooming condemn' cell favourite no longer. You'll be —— sorry it wasn't the hangman by the time we finished with you. You'll find out —— double quick there's no blasted favouritism here."

"Yes, sir," I answered the head-warder and followed a disciple warder across the length of the hall and then in through a grille gate and then up a flight of iron stairs that brought me on to a landing consisting of two sets of cages. They were steel cages, partitioned from each other by bolted steel plates, like you see in a ship. One row had steel plates in front as well; the other row had bars and wire mesh. I hoped they would put me in a cage with bars and wire mesh in front. You could see a little way out into the passage through the wire. And the all-steel cage looked somewhat cold. But my luck was out. The section-warder took me along a passage, unlocked an all-steel cage, waited for me to enter and then, without a word, slammed the steel door shut on me; and left.

I found out, when we were next unlocked, that I was in A-2 Section, the first-offenders' section, and that long-timers were kept in the all-steel cages and only short-timers were allowed in the cages with wire-fronts.

In that cage in A-2 Section I spent quite a number of years.

3

The first shop in which I worked was the printers. I was there for over a year, I think. And what I learnt about printing in the

Swartklei Great Prison has stood me in good stead through the years. I learnt something of everything. First I was in charge of the paper-store. Because the warder thought I would be more intelligent than the general run of convicts, he put me in charge of classifying and issuing the various kinds of paper. Double demy azure laid; 48 cream laid; 60 cream laid; quarto octavo; double-large post; I.V.P. double-crown. A little later, when he found out that I was less intelligent than the general run of convict, the warder put me in charge of scrubbing the floor with a short-handled brush. From there I progressed to helping to lock up the formes in the chases, and arranging the packing on the croppers and the cylinders and feeding, and working the cutting-machine, and finally – and this I showed most promise at – comping. At the end I became reasonably efficient at hand-setting. It was all hand-setting. We used to set by hand, run off on the machines and then dis the type by hand. We printed – oh, practically everything. We printed hundreds of different kinds of forms in use in the Prisons and other Government departments. All our work had the imprint, P.C.P., and the number and the date. We also turned out religious tracts and booklets, and hymn-books. And annual reports of charitable institutions.

The system in the Swartklei Great Prison is for the first offenders to be kept separate from men with previous convictions while in the cells; but in the workshops there is no segregation. Needless to say, I was considerably more interested in the old lags (until I got sick of them) than I was in the first offenders. The hardened criminals, their talk and their ways, fascinated me. It was all so different from what I had been used to.

I got a bad reputation at the start, with the warders and the first offender convicts, because whenever I got the chance I would slip away and have a chat with criminals who had long strings of previous convictions. And on exercise in the yard, half-an-hour each morning and half-an-hour each night, I would choose as my half-section in the exercise ring any hardened recidivist whose conversation was colourful. As I have said, this practice brought me into disrepute, at the start. But afterwards there wasn't any more comment on my behaviour. The concensus of opinion seemed to be that, in my association with the lowest kind of gaol-bird, I had gravitated to my own level.

4

Colourful conversation. The way these old lags talked, the blue-coats and the near blue-coats. Their vivid phraseology sounded like poetry to me. It was incredible that here, in South Africa, there was actually a class of person who spoke an argot that was known only to his kind. Boob slang, they called it. Boob, and not jug, being the Swartklei prison word for a prison. The name for a warder was a screw. You never heard any other name for him. Shoes they called daisies; trousers, rammies. A cell was a peter. "I forgot it up in my peter." For "the going is difficult" they would say "the game is hook." Or crook. Or onkus. They would have clichés, like "The boys in the game are still the same." And the queer thing was that nobody outside of ex-convicts knew these expressions, while the criminal class habitually spoke no other language. And all this was going on here, in South Africa, and I had lived to the age of twenty years, and I had never known that there really was a world such as this, here in our midst, with its own criminal parlance, and its own terribly different, terribly mysterious way of life.

And the inside stories of burglaries . . . In house and store-breaking one man stays outside to keep watch – the longstall, they call him. And when the johns come he tips his pals off. "I was longstall when Snowy Fisher and Pap done that job in Jeppes. And I piped what looks like two johns coming round the johnny horner. And I gives them the office to edge it. But something had gone hook with the soup. (Dynamite). The soup spills before they got it in the hole in the safe. (The dynamite exploded prematurely.) And so Snowy Fisher comes out of the window, all right, with half his rammies burnt off him, right into the arms of them two johns. But it's shutters for Pap. All of him that come out of the bank then was his foot, that got blowed through the fanlight. Pap never was no good with the soup. He always had his own ideas. And one of the johns pipes me and I starts ducking for a fence, and I gets over it, with the john after me – and who do you think I nearly falls on to, on the other side the fence?"

"The Governor-General?" I guessed, facetiously, "Doing a spot of illicit liquor-selling?"

"No, it wasn't the Governor-General. It wasn't the Prime Minister, neither. Nor even the Minister for Posts and Tele-grafts. It was none other than the One-Eyed Bombardier."

"You mean the Bombardier?" I asked, "The one that works in the carpenter shop?"

"Him," was the reply, "And he was all steamed up with dagga and he was as calm as you please, relieving himself standing up against the fence, not knowing that there was a job going on in that same block, and that Pap had been blowed to hell and that Snowy Fisher was pinched and that there was a john trailing me all out that very moment. 'So long, Bomb,' I shouts out, 'I got to run.' 'Wait till I finish, and I'll run with you,' he says, 'What's the gevolt?' But I got no time to tell him, what with the john's footsteps coming nearer all the time, other side of the fence. So we beats it through a dark passage the Bombardier and me, and a few minutes later we hears bang-

bang from the gun of the john that has just seen us ducking into the opening of another passage. And we runs a bit faster. But we know also that we'll get away. The john wouldn't let fly with his shooter if he didn't know he couldn't catch up with us no more. By that time it's about three o'clock in the morning.

" 'Got anywhere to sleep?' the Bombardier asks me when we goes along the railway-track on the way to Doornfontein, keeping all we can to the dark places. So I says to him, no, I can't go back to the pozzy I'm sharing with Snowy Fisher and the late Pap. Like as not the johns is already laying for me there. Looks like I'll have to go in smoke. 'Well,' the Bombardier says, 'I know a good place where you can go in smoke. Where they won't never think of looking for you, neither.' So I says I hope he don't mean the Rietfontein lazaretto. Because the Rietfontein lazaretto is out. One time, yes, it was a good pozzy. You just go along and report your dose and the quack examines you and he says, O.K. you're a danger to the public with that dose. You better come as a in-patient for treatment until we cures you. That was all-right in the old-days. The Rietfontein lazaretto was the best pozzy for going into smoke in. The johns would never nose round there. All the time you're having a easy rest, lying on the flat of your back and getting treatment for venereal disease that you've had ever since you slept with Big Polly, what has already been dead for ten years, all this time the johns is wasting petrol and getting blisters on their feet looking for you in Fordsburg or Vrededorp. But the lazaretto is crook, now. Since a detective head constable was took there for *his* dose. This john gets took there for treatment and what does he see but half-a-dozen boys what has been in smoke a long time doing a flit out the dormitory the moment he walks in.

"So I says to the Bombardier that if he knows of a place

where I can go in smoke it better be a good place. And it also better not be the Rietfontein lazaretto, or any kind of lazaretto, where a john with siph can come walking in and me flat on my back with no chance to scale out of the window. But the Bombardier says, no, the place what he knows is a good pozzy to go to smoke in. It's on a farm, the Bombardier says. 'You know what a farm is, I expect?' the Bombardier says to me, looking suspicious, as though I had never heard of a farm. So I told him that I had growed up on a farm. And that I never came to Johannesburg before I was fifteen. And that I was already turned seventeen before the first time I got pinched. I told him I wasn't like one of the Joh'burg reformatory rats that can't stay out of reform school after they passed the age of fourteen. 'Look how many young blokes go to reformatory before they is fifteen," I says to the Bombardier, "That shows you what it is to be brung up in a city, dragged up in the gutter, you might say. But with me. No, chum, with me it was different. I was brung up on a farm. So I was a long way past seventeen before the johns nabbed me. And then they wouldn't have got me, neither, if one of my pals hadn't gone and squealed on me. No, what I says is, bring up a child in the city, and he'll go wrong. Look at me. I been brought up on a farm. And I smoke dagga. And I been twice warned for the coat. And if I was brought up in a city, where would I be to-day, I'd like to know?' And the Bombardier says I would be a criminal, most likely, seeing as how a child brought up in the city had got no chances at all to learn honesty and a respect for the law.

"By this time we come to the top end of Siemert Road, just by the side of the railway-cutting, and we sits down on a piece of brown rock, feeling safe, now, with the johns the other end of town, taking Snowy Fisher to Marshall Square and Pap to the mortuary. And the Bombardier takes a piece of paper out of his pocket and tears it into the right size and then he pulls out some of the old queer and mixes some cigarette tobacco with it, and in a few minutes we are sitting as happy as you please on that rock, pulling away at that dagga-stoppie. It was good dagga. We both feels very honest. Because in between the Bombardier had let on to me that he was also brought up on a farm. And so we each tries to let the other see how much good it does one to be brought up on a farm, and we each try to sound more honest and good than the other one.

"I starts off by telling the Bombardier about all the times I done tried to look for a job of work. There was twice that I could remember for sure. But there was another time, also, that I seemed to think I had applied for a job, but I couldn't quite just remember, because I had got that time mixed up with another time when I asked Alec the Ponce if I could help him to live on the earnings of prostitution of some of the trollopes he was trailing around with. But the Bombardier said that that showed you. I had walked myself black and blue, trudging the whole country, looking for a job of honest work. And that was because I had had the good fortune to have been brung up on a farm. Then we starts talking about all the times we had tried to reform. We found we had each of us tried a whole lot of times. Me, at least twice, again. And the Bombardier more than three times.

"There was a time, too, when the Bombardier had gone about making a clean breast of things. A salvation army captain had spoke to the Bombardier once, just before he was coming out of boob after his fourth stretch, and the salvation army captain had said to the Bombardier to go out that time and make a clean breast of it. 'Go out of the boob, my man,' the salvation army captain says to the Bombardier, 'and own up as you done wrong, and look the world in the face.' But before the

Bombardier can go on with his story, when he passes me the dagga-smoke again, I remembers when a parson said the same thing to me. So I also decides right on the turn to go round and make a clean breast of it. That was one of the times in my life what I told you about when I went to look for a job of work. Not when I seen Alec the Ponce about doing a spot of poncing, but the real first time in my life when I went to look for a job. I was forty-two years old then. And this parson bloke had said to me, 'Don't try and conceal your past,' he says, 'For your past will catch up with you, and just when you think you've pulled the wool over your employer's eyes, you'll find yourself dropped in the muck.' I could see that this parson had got the game pretty well measured up. I never laugh at a parson. I've found as there is lots of things as a parson knows that you don't give him credit for at the time and then afterwards you find if you had done what he worked out for you you would have clicked. I have even thought perhaps when I get out of boob this time I can go to a parson and get him to work out the lay of a crib for me. Perhaps I can even go and crack my next safe dressed as a parson. Only, if I get pinched, Gawd, how won't the boys in the awaiting trial yard rib me, me turning up charged with safe-blowing, and in a parson's suit and with a round collar and a hymn-book. I can just picture a parson sitting in the corner of a cell on his hymn-book, smoking dagga.

"But I followed that parson's advice. I decided to go straight and to work honest-like, and if the johns come and try to put my pot on with the boss, what a laugh they'll get when he knows my rep as good as the johns does. So I looks in the Star situations vacant and I pipe a advertisement, wanted, a care-taker for a ladies social club premises, must be sober, light duties. A skinny moll with specs opens the door and gives me a

39

dekko. 'I suppose you'll do,' she says, 'You been drinking a lot, I suppose, on your last job, and that's how they fired you?' But I says, no, all I had to drink in five years was prison-soup. Soup with carrots in, I says. 'Ho, so you are a ex-convict?' she says, 'Do come in.' She makes me sit down and gives me a cup of tea. 'Is it really as dreadful in prison as what reports of it is?' she asks, very inquisitive. And I says, no, it's all right if you can get a bit, now and again. And a dagga stompie some- times. And on Christmas eves there is a concert, I says. And one Sunday every month you gets pepper in your stew.

"The skinny moll with the specs and the high collar gets real interested. 'Tell me,' she says, 'is it really as bad about the — about the — I mean, you didn't say a bit of *bun*, did you?' Then I twigs. 'Oh, *that*,' I says, 'missus, don't let that upset you, missus. What you expect a man to do, locked up night after night, and no women? And that going on for years. Not even a kafir-woman. Or a coolie-woman pushing a vegetable-cart. Not a smell of a woman. For years and years. Well, a man is only human, aint he? You can't expect a man to be more than what flesh and blood can stand, can you?' And she said, no, she thought not, and she said she was real worried, and she had been for a long time, and the other molls in her club, also, about unnatural sex acts as men gets up to, when they is locked away by themselves. And I says there is nothing unnatural about it, and I couldn't feel there was anything unnatural about me, even though I am sure I have had more men as what she has had women. And she just shakes her head and says as I can start right away, and have I told her everything. So I remembers the advice the parson bloke give me, and I come my whole guts, clean, and I thinks, now if a john comes and blabs to my em- ployer about my previouses, won't that john get a earful.

"So I pulls my whole rep to the skinny moll. 'I been in boob

40

seven times', I says, putting in a extra one for good measure, in case the johns come round and tells her I done six stretches. 'And I smokes dagga,' I says. 'And I am rotten with syphilis,' I says. 'And I also wants to tell you —' "

But at that moment the bell rang, and the exercise period was over, and so I had to fall in, without hearing the rest of this blue-coat's story. So I never knew what the upshot was of his attempt at reformation, or whether he did go into smoke on that farm. The whole story ended just like that, in mid-air, leaving him sitting on that stone near the Siemert cutting, smoking dagga with the One-Eyed Bombardier. But I knew I could go back to him any time, and he would continue with that story from the point where he had left off, if I had asked him to. Or else he would have told me a brand new story, starting just from anywhere and ending up nowhere – exactly like his own life was. And what was wonderful to me was the fact that any blue-coat, or any convict who had served five or six fairly long sentences in prison, could tell stories in exactly the same strain. You don't go to prison, over and over again, just for nothing. And if you don't gather any moss in this way you certainly learn a lot of queer things. And so I was fascinated with the talk of these old prison hands, through whose lives there was threaded purple drama, which they hardly ever recognised as such. The situations were always old. A robbery and a getaway and a john round the corner. An l a girl, some-times. And the girls in the lives of these hardened criminals seemed to me to be very colourful creatures – perhaps because these blue-coats knew so little about women, really, being isolated from all women for such long periods on end: and perhaps, therefore, in retrospect, women seemed to them romantic and glamorous, with the most squalid prostitute becoming endowed with all sorts of dark mystery. And it must be remembered that I, too, knew very little about women. But at the age of twenty I was most anxious to learn.

Anyway, in one story the girl in the crook's life would be somebody tender and wistful (I would picture her as graceful and slender and with dark hair and eyes) and she would be gazing out into the silence for always, waiting for a lover who would come back to her no more. Or else the girl would be false to her man (a platinum blonde, I imagined, with a small mouth, ungenerous, and with a hard glitter in her blue eyes) and the moment her man got arrested she would run off to live with the john who had pinched him.

But there they were, these convicts who had done seven, eight, a dozen stretches. Touch a man like that anywhere, and a story would flow from him like blood from a wound. They were no longer human beings. They were no longer people, or living creatures in the ordinary sense of the word. They were merely battered receptacles of stories; tarnished and rusted containers out of which strange tales issued, like djinns out of magic bottles.

And so I got a bad name in the Swartklei Great Prison, right from the first few weeks of my having been moved from the death-house to A2 Section. I got this bad name because I was so often seen in the company of the most depraved kind of criminal. And it was observed that I really enjoyed being in the company of this type of unregenerate scoundrel, because I always listened with such grave interest to what he had to say, and I always laughed at the right places, and I also, in time, began consciously, to acquire the blue-coat's mode of speech.

To me the first offenders' section was like a small and narrow-minded village. The blue-coat's spirit was the city.

To be locked up in a prison and to be misunderstood by those about you has got to it certain very bitter features. Especially if you are young and you have gaiety in your nature.

Chapter 3

DURING THE TIME I was in the Swartklei Great Prison I smoked dagga on only rare occasions, and I never went in for homosexual practices – the thought of which, indeed, was most abhorrent to me. All right, it was priggish of me to have clung in that way to the outer garments of respectability, but the fact remains that I was only, after all, a first offender. Since those days I have discovered that in the world outside prison homosexuality exists to a degree that would probably be an eye-opener to the blue-coats. And because so many people I know either are, or are suspected of being, sodomites and lesbians, and because perversions of this description do not seem to have attached to them the odium that I fancied they were invested with a quarter of a century ago, I suppose that I nowadays extend to such things a theoretical tolerance which I did not have while I was still in prison.

I never had any prejudice against dagga. Why I didn't smoke this weed to any great extent was (1) because it was rather scarce and (2) because it did not seem to have the same exhilarating effect on me as it had on the regular rookers.

I had not been in prison very long before I came across dagga-smoking. I have since learnt that dagga is a herb, that its scientific name is Indian hemp (cannabis indica) and that it is closely allied botanically to hashish, and that it is smoked, in one form or another, practically throughout the world. But all I had known about dagga, before I went to prison, was that it was a kind of weed that was smoked by Bushmen and the more degraded kind of native, and that it drove you mad. Before going to prison I was unaware of the fact that dagga was also smoked by white members of the underworld.

During the time I was in the Great Prison, dagga-smoking was not so much a habit among the old offenders as it was by way of being a venerable institution. Dagga was smuggled into the prison in various ways, and the price for it was high, a single stoppie of dagga being reckoned as the equivalent of twenty doppies (or a whole week's ration) of tobacco. To be found in possession of dagga was a serious prison offence: the first time you were caught you got solitary confinement and an extra three months on of your sentence; if you were caught after that you could get lashes. But in spite of the heavy penalties attached to the smoking of this weed, (hardly a month passing without some convict or other going to solitary for it), the dagga habit was pretty strongly entrenched among the regular gaol-birds.

They had all sorts of names for it, "boom" being the most common. They also called it "Nellie," or "grass," or "voëls," or "American green leaf," or "pappegaai." They also spoke of it as "the weed," or "the herb," or "the queer stuff" (although this latter appellation is more usually applied to methylated spirits). I also remember the word "ashes" for it (a corruption, I thought, of hashish). Anyway, you can tell by the number of names they had for it that "boom" held a fairly important place in prison life.

I have never come across anybody who smoked dagga neat. Perhaps because it is too scarce, a luxury smoke. At all events, the green leaves are first crushed in the palm of the hand and are then mixed with a certain quantity of tobacco, according to some secret formula that is supposed to be in the possession of only one or two habitual rookers. The mixture is then rolled into a cigarette, the brown toilet-paper supplied in prison being used for this purpose. There is some superstition to the effect that dagga hasn't got any effect on you if you smoke it in white paper. The dagga cigarette is now ready (the "zol", they call it), and the rookers gather round in a circle. Each man takes two or three quick puffs at the burning dagga-cigarette, inhaling the smoke as deep down into his lungs as it will go, to get the maximum kick from it, and then passes it on to the next man in the circle. Each rooker, as he gets the zol, comments on its quality. He will say "It's a good mix", meaning that the person who blended the dagga with the tobacco, in rolling the cigarette, used the right proportions of dagga and tobacco. Or he will say, "There's too much leaf in it, and not enough head." Or he will say, "This is real Swaziland boom" – meaning, thereby, the best dagga procurable. Or, again, "This has got too much blasted pitte in it." And so on, into infinity. For there is no end to what you can say about the quality of a dagga smoke. Between good and bad dagga there are a myriad gradations.

When a man hangs on to a zol for longer than the two or three quick puffs he is supposed to take, and forgets to pass it round, the other rookers in the circle will start getting impatient. "Don't put your name and address on it," they will say to him. Or "Don't put your boob number on it." Or – strongest injunction of all – "Don't put your string of previous convictions on that zol."

As I have said, I never smoked dagga to any extent. Once in a while I would take a pull or two at a zol, more for the reason that I didn't want to be thought to be acting in a superior way than because of any enjoyment I got out of it. And, of course, just for the hell of it, just because dagga-smoking was regarded in the outside world as representing the nadir of criminal degeneration – for that reason I would get a strange thrill out of the thought that I was smoking dagga. The popular attitude towards dagga-smoking, making of it something mysteriously sinful and raising it to the level of a secret vice indulged in only by the most abandoned of mortals, served as a challenge to me. Dagga was invested for me with all the romantic associations that the sound of the word "absinthe" had, for instance, for people who were fascinated by the word "art" in terms of the French decadents at the end of the last century. I got a thrill out of the thought that I was smoking dagga, and not out of the act of smoking dagga.

But with the rookers it is different. They tell you beautiful things about what dagga does to them. And they all warn you against smoking dagga, assuring you that in the end it drives you mad. But whether they got this information out of the newspapers, or whether it is knowledge gradually being acquired by each rooker through introspective self-analysis, is something on which I can't offer an opinion.

I had read "The Count of Monte Cristo", and I had remembered that chapter in which somebody is introduced to the witched splendour of hashish-smoke. And so, when the rookers told me that boom affected them in this way, or in that way, I knew that they were genuinely susceptible to the narcotic influence of this drug, and in my isolation I envied them. I have never been able to understand why it is that, of all the people I have known who smoked dagga, I have been the only one that does not get affected by it. I have heard the view expressed – and I repeat it for what it is worth – and that is that in my natural condition I am so peculiar and my thoughts so erratic that it is difficult for people to believe that I am *not* under the influence of dagga half the time.

The first time I heard convicts talk about dagga they referred to it as "boom." I wanted to know why. They said, well, you know, "boom" is the Afrikaans word for a tree. Granted, I said, but so what? Then they said it meant tree of knowledge. They said that if you smoked dagga you knew everything that there was in the world, and even a lot that wasn't. They had quite a variety of expressions meaning "to be under the influence of dagga." They would call it, obviously enough, "being under the influence." But their favourite word for it was "blue". "To be blue", in Swartklei Great Prison slang, didn't mean melancholy. It didn't mean, "When I am blue and you are far away." If somebody said to you, "Man, ek is blou," it meant that his mind was heavy with gaudy dreams. If a man said,"I was blue when I done it," he didn't mean that he was out of sorts, or that inclemency on the part of the weather had made him turn blue, but that simply when he had done whatever he was referring to – stolen a bicycle or chopped his mother – it wasn't he that was doing it but the dagga.

"Blue" was the most usual way of talking about one being under the spell of dagga, but there were other expressions, like "geswael", "boomed up", "herbed" and "soaped". (Here I find myself writing in the past tense, as though about things that have been and will never come again – as though all that boob talk and all those boob practices of two decades ago have vanished for ever from the knowledge of man. Perhaps they have, I don't know. Perhaps there isn't a boob any more, either, in Swartklei. Perhaps it is the dagga, insidiously, that makes me write of it in the past: seeking to array itself in that glamour, that pale nostalgia and fragile loveliness, that resides in a time that has gone by.)

"The tree of knowledge," a blue-coat would say, when the zol had gone the rounds for the last time and was burnt out so short that you couldn't get a pull out of the brown-paper any more, even if you held it to your lips with a needle, because the stompie wasn't long enough to be held in your fingers, "The tree of knowledge. When I is blue like what I is now, then I says you can maar keep me locked up in the old boob as long as you blerrie well like."

"What do you want to pick on us for, Boet? What you want to say for we keep you locked up? It's not us, man. We ain't keeping you here. It's the walls and the screws (warders) and the john what pinched you. Why blame us blokes?"

"The tree of knowledge," the blue-coat would repeat, "Give me a few pulls every morning with the mealie-pap and I'll tell the Governor he can go and bugger himself, every morning with the mealie-pap."

"When I am blue, like now," another convict would say, "Like now, mind you. I dunno how the hell I'll feel say lock-up time. But the way I feel right here and now, sitting on my backside against this – what the —— hell am I sitting against, anyway? –"

"Against a bone-sack," his pal would explain, nonchalantly.

"Well, I won't change this bone-sack for a – for a what now –" and his voice would trail away into the void.

As a matter of fact, most of the dagga-parties I attended were held in the bone-yard. The real place for smoking dagga was, of course, inside a cell with a whole lot together. But they had community cells only for the old offenders. The first offenders, as I have explained, slept alone, in single cages. But the bone-yard wasn't a bad place. It consisted of a stack of bones of domestic and wild animals on which the flesh was often still rotting. Behind this pile of bones were more bones, but in sacks, dozens and dozens of sacks of bones, and they were arranged in a rough semi-circle. In the small area between the semi-circle of bones in sacks and the pile of unsacked bones a number of convicts would ensconce themselves on such occasions as they wished to indulge in a surreptitious dagga-smoke in the yard. The stench of the bones kept the warders at a reasonable distance. If, in spite of the stink of rotting bones and putrescent flesh the warder came too near, because he was too insensitive to be put off by unpleasant odours, it was easy to slip away through the openings between the piles of sacks, and just pretend that you were going to the lavatory, or that the head had slipped off your hammer (if you were working in the stone-yard) and that you were taking it to the carpenters' shop for repairs, or that you had come there because there seemed to be a stink like something dead, and don't you think he should report it to the Governor, meneer? Didn't meneer perhaps think, with that funny smell about, that the body of some prison officer might be lying there under those sacks? Didn't meneer smell something dead – a smell like a dead warder, perhaps, meneer, who had been murdered by some of the stone-yard convicts?

The excuse you would make for being in the bone-yard would vary considerably – depending on how blue you were. I have noticed that when convicts are blue and they enter into conversation with warders, they can tell the most extra-ordinary stories – and convincingly. But the chief advantage of smoking amongst all those decaying bones (they were used for fertilizer and in button-making) was the stink of the bones. The higher the bones stank to heaven, the better we liked it. The stink of the bones completely disguised the pungent and very individualistic smell of burning dagga. It wasn't enough, if they wanted to charge you with smoking dagga, for the warder to report that he smelt the acrid fumes of boom, crackling in his nostrils: he had actually to catch you dead to rights with a quantity of dagga on you, a couple of shreds, two leaves and

49

a pip being sufficient. And so if a warder advanced on the bone-stacks, and he seemed to be determined to come right inside the circle of charmed stinks, the convict who happened to have the stoppie at that moment would crush the fire out of it and retain it in his possession as long as possible, in the hope of being able to light it on a later occasion. If the warder still came on, it would be that convict's duty, then, to destroy the stoppie. The most usual way was to unwrap the brown paper quickly and swallow what was left of the mix of tobacco and boom. When a convict did that – when he ate the stuff – they said he would remain blue for weeks.

Just a few generalities about boom:

They say there are three kinds of education: a classical education, a scientific education, and dagga. They say you can acquire a good education through studying books in universities, but you get even better educated through smoking boom in boob. And they believe that, too. At one time a gentleman from Pretoria was permitted to give religious instruction in the chapel once a week during the lunch-hour to such convicts as wished to attend his little meetings. It was all done on a voluntary basis. It was an addition to the regular Sunday services, conducted by the ministers of the various denominations. Among the few who attended these services was an old rooker known as Bul. The gentleman who organised these weekly lunch-hour meetings used to appoint two convicts, each session, to give short, edifying talks on the Bible. One day it was old Bul's turn to talk. "I don't know nothing about the Bible," he announced, "But what's inside me does."

What was inside him was a sizeable volume of dagga fumes. And he genuinely believed that that was all he needed to be able to talk authoritatively on the Bible or any other subject under the sun. Maybe he was right. I don't know. I only know that shortly afterwards those little lunch-hour classes in religious instruction were abandoned.

They say that the best way to smoke dagga is to draw it through water in a hole made in the ground, in a "grond-aar", like the Bushman smokes it. You kneel down on the ground and pull at a reed. There seems to be something peculiarly fitting in this posture: making low obeisance to the Tree of Knowledge: kneeling on the ground in the presence of ancient wisdom. But I never saw dagga smoked that way while I was in the prison. With all those warders about, one couldn't make such elaborate preparations; one could not observe the proper ritual as prescribed by the Bushmen. But they told me a story of the old days. It was something that happened before my time, before they had walled in the back of the mat-shop and that side of the prison ended in an excavation and a barbed wire fence patrolled by outside warders. Anyway, somebody made a grond-aar in a spot behind a bunker of excavated rock. The convicts who knew about it would go there, one by one, kneel down behind the bunker and in front of the aar, and pull away through a bit of leaky wood that had been hollowed into a tube in the carpenters' shop. One of the warders on outside duty observed this somewhat singular activity. He was a raw recruit and ignorant of prison ways. So he put down his gun, climbed through the fence, and went across to a convict who was kneeling down with his face to the ground – surprising the convict from the rear.

"What you doing here?" the warder demanded.

Taken unaware, and blue from the boom, the convict blurted out, "Smoking dagga, meneer."

The recruit hadn't been in the prison service very long, but he had heard about dagga-smoking while he was still training in the depot, and he had been told what terrible stuff dagga was, and so he was interested. The rooker's frankness (because he was blue) in owning up to what he was doing, also contributed to taking the recruit off his guard.

"But how can you do such a thing?" the recruit enquired, remembering what he had learnt by rote in the training depot, "Smoking that awful, habit-forming drug called Indian hemp, that drives you mad?"

"Easy," the convict answered, "You just kneels down here, like this, and you pull up the smoke through this piece of stick."

The recruit's curiosity got the better of him. Next thing, he was also kneeling on the ground, inhaling deeply, the pale blue smoke wreathed fragilely about his face and curving sharply into his lungs. And at that very moment, of course, the headwarder had to come on his rounds. It just had to be. And the head-warder, coming around the bunker, from behind, was confronted by what was to him the incredible sight of a warder-recruit, his rifle on the other side of the barbed-wire fence, kneeling down on the ground, with a convict standing next to him, keeping watch, and the air fragrant with the acrid sweetness of burning boom.

"What the hell's this?" the head-warder roared.

The recruit in his turn, also taken unaware and also blue, replied, still in a kneeling posture, and with his head still to the ground.

"I am smoking dagga, sir."

The recruit was fired out of the prison service immediately. And because it would have created too much of a scandal if it became known that a warder in the Swartklei Great Prison had been discharged for smoking dagga – and out of a grond-aar, of all things – the matter wasn't brought to court. He wasn't charged with smoking dagga on duty – which would have meant a trial before a magistrate and subsequent un-pleasant publicity. Instead, the recruit was merely brought be-fore the prison Governor on the accusation that he had deserted his post while on outside guard and so he was chucked out of the prison service.

The story of boom is a long and – to me – entrancing story. They say that it is good for asthma, and that it is habit-forming, and that it drives you mad. When I was in the Swartklei there were old convicts, grown grey in crime, who could remember the old days in the Transvaal when dagga-smoking was not illegal. You could buy a parcel of dagga over a grocer's coun-ter, like you would buy butter or boot-polish. But gradually, because so many of the people who committed crimes turned out to be dagga-rookers, dagga got into disrepute with the authorities and somebody brought in a law about it.

But it's time I changed the subject. My going on and on, in this way, writing about dagga, starts making me think that it might really be habit-forming . . .

2

A typical day in the Great Prison – what is it like?

You are awakened about 5.30 a.m. by the rising gong, a raucous clangour that reverberates throughout the wings and corridors of the prison, as though to set a tone of nerve-wracked ill-humour for the rest of the day. You awaken, there-fore, and you rise. You take off the blue jean three-quarter length night-shirt that you have been wearing and you pull on your stockings and your short-sleeved shirt (prison-made out of a coarse, scratchy material that is a source of everlasting irritation to the skin) and you pull on your knicker-bockers. Then you feel under the top part of the numnah mat lying on the floor for your boots, which have served you during the night as a pillow. When you have got your boots and jacket on, you are dressed.

Next, you start folding your blankets. There is a special way of doing this: I can't describe it, but it's very clever. The first week you are in prison you get shown, every morning, by a cleaner-convict (his job is that of cleaner: he is not really cleaner than other convicts, either in respect of his person or morally) how to fold and arrange your blankets so that they make a square, compact bundle. Next week, and from then onwards, you have got to make up your blankets yourself, the prison regulations demanding that the final result shall be a tight, squarely-folded bundle, neatly perched on the rolled-up numnah stood on end against the wall. The Governor and the chief warder, accompanied by the section officer, pass through the corridors once a day, glancing in at the cells, and if everything isn't spick and span, the floor polished and the blankets accurately perched, and the tin spoon and pannikin shining, the Governor draws the attention of the section officer to that particular cell, and the occupant, at that moment probably sawing away in the timber yard, has his name booked down for solitary confinement for the next three days.

By the time you have folded and stacked your blankets and you have got your jacket on, the section warder is coming down the corridor unlocking the cell-doors. You grab up your sanitary pail and stand to attention in front of the door. The door is unlocked. "Môre, meneer," you shout, in terms of the regulations, and you go flying down the corridor to try and get a place on the open latrine. After that you empty your pail, wash it under a tap, scour it quickly with a piece of brick, try and get some sort of a wash yourself, and then dash back to your cell.

By this time the cleaners are coming round with the break-fast, a dixie of mealie-pap and a ladle of black, bitter coffee, which you receive in your pannikin. After you have eaten you rush back to the wash-house to clean your spoon and pannikin (the washing of the dixies being the work of the kitchen-cleaners) and you stand in front of your cage, waiting for the next bell, which always seem to ring before you are ready.

The whole prison then files out to work – with the exception of the cleaners, the three library assistants, the cooks, the reception stores hands and other convicts whose activities are confined to work inside the prison.

In single file, section after section, clattering down the iron stairs, tramping along the corridors and through the grey, bleak hall, hundreds of convicts march out every morning, with the second bell, to their various workshops. There are a few prized jobs in the prison, like being a hospital orderly, when you sleep in one of the wards, on a bed with sheets and a mattress, and you wear a white shirt and hospital blues, like the patients. After you have been doing time in the sections for a number of years, and you get pneumonia or some such disease, and you are taken to the prison hospital, you feel so lost and strange, in civilised surroundings, that you can't believe the bed and the sheets are real, and you feel you must walk about on tip-toe, and that you musn't touch anything. It's not the delirium from your high fever that gives you these queer obsessions: it's just the incredible alteration in your circumstances – from being locked up nightly in a steel cage and sleeping on a numnah mat on a concrete floor, with your boots as a pillow, and being fed on coarse fare – to the elegance of having a blue flannel suit to wear, and a bed to sleep in, and getting nourishing food served on an enamel plate instead of in a tin dixie. I have seen men in hospital, in the first stage of convalescence, awakening to the luxury of their surroundings and bursting into tears.

Other "soft" jobs are semi-clerical positions in places like the stores, where you have a lot to do with warders who are really book-keepers and clerks, and who are not so narrowly concerned with the rigid observance of the rules of prison discipline, and who leave long cigarette-ends for you to pick up. A job in the kitchen was also looked on as something to aspire to, extra food, and all that. But the thought of having to work all day long in an atmosphere of greasy steam, with having more to eat as the only perquisite of office repelled me. I was on several occasions offered a job in the kitchen. I refused each time.

The prized jobs went by bribery and influence. That was how I got into hospital once, as an orderly, for a brief period. I bribed a long-term convict in the hospital, who had a lot of influence with the warders, to put in a good word for me with a prominent member of the hospital staff. I gave this convict ten rations of tobacco, which I had smuggled in to me through a warder, a friend in the outside world supplying the money for it. But I didn't stay in the hospital as an orderly very long. It was a job highly thought of by the boob-heads. So they used cunning as well as straight bribery, and after a short while I got pitched out.

Through the hall we marched across a long, narrow space, surrounded by high walls. This space, only a few yards wide, (so that the sun rarely shone into it), and about a hundred yards long – or fifty yards long: I have never been any good at judging distance – was known as the first offenders' yard. Here the first offenders spent their Saturday afternoons and Sundays, in between being locked up in the cells. It was a queer thing how hard they seemed to make it for the first offenders: first compelling them to sleep in small, steel cages instead of the regular prison cells, and then making them exercise in what was by far the worst and unhealthiest yard in the prison. Perhaps the idea was to frighten first offenders off, to make things so unpleasant for them that they wouldn't want to come around again.

From the first offenders' yard we went through some iron railings and walked down a passage that would bring us into what looked like a football field.

All along the route were warders shouting out commands at intervals. These commands were for the sake of maintaining general discipline. They hardly ever bore reference to any specific circumstance. They were of this nature: "Pick up your step, there!" and "Button up your —— jacket!" and "Stop talking, you!" and "Get a blasted shove on!" and "Don't look at me like that, or I'll charge you!" Meaningless remarks, addressed at nobody in particular, but that sounded very ferocious until you got used to them. I should say that it would take, on an average, about three years to get used to that form of procedure on the part of the warders – addressing blood-curdling threats and stern injunctions at nobody in particular. After that, bellowed invective had no effect on you. In this high-walled yard the various spans would be formed. The convicts would break out of file and each would go and take up his accustomed position in the ranks of the workshop to which he had been allocated. The trades-warder of each shop would stand on a raised part of the field and the number of convicts reporting for work for the day would be charged to him, the chief warder being present to participate in the checking, and after the trades warder had said "All correct, sir", and had saluted the chief, he would say, "Forward, Carpenters' Span," or "Brush-Shop Span", or "Blacksmiths' Span" – whichever shop he was in charge of – and we would march forward, in fours, through the mortuary-gate which, (I assume through faulty architecture) was also the gate that provided egress from the prison building into the workshops' wing.

When a man died in prison, either naturally or through the rope, he was first taken to the mortuary for dissection. After that, with a piece of sacking thrown over him, he would be carted by wheel-barrow through the mortuary-gate and into the workshops' yard, where a truck waited to remove him for burial. The dead and the living alike, leaving the confines of the penal section of the prison, had to make their way through the mortuary-gate.

It was a strain on my nerves, having to pass through that mortuary-gate, with its unpleasant associations, four times a day. One day I observed an Irishman, who was marching immediately in front of me, making the sign of the cross over his breast and forehead. I imitated his actions. I found that it was strangely comforting to cross oneself, marching through the mortuary-gate; and from then onwards, for years and years, regularly, four times a day on working days, whenever I passed through the gate of the mortuary I would make the sign of the cross. I would recommend any convict now in the Swartklei Prison who happens to read this to do the same thing. You can't go wrong with it. The stench of death constantly overhangs that small area between the mortuary-gate and the gallows' tower. I don't know what has put that stink there. I don't know whether it is actually the stink of corpses (brought through there from the gallows or the hospital), that lies over that part of the boob; or whether it is the smell of the fear of so many convicts that have passed through there during the course of the years: and that the ground has been impregnated with these fears: for mass-fear stinks just like death, the stink of carrion; or whether it is only the odour of decaying bones that the wind wafts from the bone-yard, which is not far from the mortuary.

I don't know how that stink gets there. But it is a frightening and depressing stink. And making the sign of the cross helps a lot.

In front of whatever shop the span is working in, a halt is made and the number of convicts is checked again. (In the course of a day, between the workshops and the sections, the convicts in the Swartklei Great Prison are checked fifteen times. That's how conscientious the authorities are about nobody leaving the place unofficially.)

Then you go into the shop and you work. That's all there is to it.

If you are working on a sedentary job, like in the book-binders or the tailors' shop, you are allowed half-an-hour's exercise, walking up and down the yard, before and after work each day. But if you have got a non-sedentary job, such as blacksmith or in the stone-yard, then, naturally, you get all the exercise you want on the job itself.

At lunch time the bell rings again. The same procedure is gone through once more. Falling in and marching; and the checking and counter-checking. And then you get inside your cage in the section, up-stairs, and you get your food – a dish of carrot-soup, mostly. An hour later you go back to work. And at about five o'clock you fall in again: you have a short working day so that the trades-warder shouldn't have to be on duty during phenomenally long hours. You get your supper – a kind of mealie-meal soup and a hunk of bread, and you are locked up again for the night, and the day is over. The electric light stays on for an hour or so, so you can read for a while before going to sleep. By the way, that mealie-meal soup, with onions in, too, sometimes, is vile smelling stuff. Nobody tries to eat more than once. And you only try and eat it that once because you wouldn't listen to all the warnings you got about it. That pint of soup is supplied religiously every night, each convict holding out his dixie and receiving the soup from a ladle and then putting the dixie out in front of his door again, without touching the contents. This formality is gone through every night because the regulations insist that a convict shall not decline to accept his food. It doesn't matter what he does with it afterwards. But when it is supplied to him he has got to take it. But the bread is good.

Oh, and there is another, and rather more serious, formality that I forgot to mention. And that is the search. You are searched regularly every time you come in from the shops into the section. You aren't searched coming out – because what the hell is there for you to bring out of a prison-cage, anyway? But coming into the section is a different thing. Because there are all sorts of illicit articles, manufactured in the work-shops, that you can smuggle into the section – "bottle in" is the term employed. You can bring in dagga. Tobacco. Writing-paper. A boot-brush. A newspaper. Bootpolish. Matches. A length of candle: so that you can go on reading in your cage surreptitiously after the lights are turned out. A host of things, depending on your needs and on your imaginative capacity to think out a new line of product to bottle into the section. To prevent this smuggling, the search has been instituted. The ordinary search is quite simple. It takes place twice a day. Each time you pass through that mortuary-gate, on your way back to the section, you break rank and go up to one or other of a line of about thirty warders. You can't get through that yard without having had some warder or other search you. You simply go up to a warder (you can pick the warder you want to search you, provided that you are not too obvious about making the choice) and you stand to attention a pace away from him with your arms laterally extended, holding your red-spotted handkerchief dangling from one hand and your hat in the other. The warder passes his hand over your clothes, up and down, and the job is done. He jerks this thumb over his shoulder and you push off.

When a strip-search is ordered, the procedure differs in a few details. You still come up to the warder, with your arms stretched out, but with your jacket and pants off. You stand facing the warder in only a very short shirt and he feels all over you, to make sure that you have hidden nothing on any part of your person. Then he goes through your jacket and pants in a very methodical fashion, and he also examines your boots. It is in the course of a strip-search that most unauthorised articles are discovered. The punishment varies, from about two years for carrying a fire-arm or about three months for having dagga on you, to three days' solitary confinement, with loss of privileges and decrease in remission of sentence, for carrying tobacco on a non-smoking day.

You get solitary on spare diet for having any unauthorised article on you – unauthorised meaning practically anything you have besides the prison garb you stand up in. Next to tobacco on a non-smoking day, the commonest unauthorised article is a tinder-box. Every convict who smokes carries a tinder-box with him as a matter of course. Else how is he going to light up? It is a serious offence to be caught in possession of matches. But throughout the decades the convicts in the Swartklei Great Prison have known how to solve the problem of providing a light for a smoke. It's all very simple. You need a small wooden box, a little larger than a thimble, and it has got to have a lid. Boxes for this purpose are manufactured in large quantity in the blacksmiths', fitters' and carpenters' shops. They will sell you a box like that for a couple of smokes. Inside this box you put a piece of burnt rag, the tinder: it has been found, incidentally, that a blue-jean night-shirt makes the best kind of tinder; hence the frequent disappearance of this garment from a convict's cell while he is out at work: throughout one whole winter I was compelled to sleep without a night-shirt, and for this reason. All you need after that is a small steel disc, about three quarters of an inch (or less) in diameter and perforated with two holes for a piece of string to go through – of a type manufactured in the blacksmiths' shop in large quantities, also, and sold for as little as one smoke. You pick up a bit of flint in the yard (emery-stone is much better, of course) and you hold one end of the looped string between your teeth and the other end caught in your bent thumb, and you set the wheel a·spinning, like an Afrikaans child's "woer-woer", and you bring the piece of stone into contact with the spinning steel wheel, holding it in your left hand, with the tinder-box in such a position as to catch the sparks that shoot off, and in a couple of seconds you are rewarded with the tinder being alight.

You can get a light from a tinder-box in this way in a few seconds, depending on your efficiency in spinning the wheel. And the box, wheel and stone, carried in a cloth bag (manufactured in the tailors' shop and retailed at less than a smoke) together take up less space than an ordinary match-box. As I have said, every convict in the Great Prison who smokes carries a tinder-box as a matter of course. (How else can you get a light?) And although the manufacture and use of tinder-boxes are to a large extent connived at by the warders, nevertheless, if you are searched and found in possession of a tinder-box, you are charged and are liable to three day's solitary confinement on spare diet, with loss of privileges and loss of a certain amount of sentence-remission.

You were allowed to smoke only on exercise and on alternate days of the week, every other day being a non-smoking day. And most of the convictions before the Governor were on charges connected with smoking. If you smoke one day, it is difficult not to smoke next day. Accordingly, in the clothbag, along with the tinder outfit, smokers would also carry whatever tobacco they had on non-smoking days. You fastened the little bag between your legs, high up. The warder was not supposed to feel there. He was supposed to respect your private parts. He could only search you between your legs in the presence of a superior officer and at a formal strip search. Hence, if there was anything you wanted to bottle out of one part of the prison into another, the only. safe place was in that small bag fastened between your legs with a piece of string. But there were a couple of warders who, ignorantly or through malice, did not observe the proprieties in this respect. These warders were known to the convicts, and it was noteworthy that in the row of warders lined up for search twice a day these particular warders did not receive much of a clientele. The only convicts who went to stand in front of these warders for searching were convicts who carried nothing fastened between their legs: or else they were pansies, and liked having a warder pass his hands all over their bodies.

I have talked about what happens on working days. From Saturday lunch time until Monday morning you had leisure. The routine then was rather different. When you came up the stairs for lunch on Saturdays there was an unusual amount of activity at the section-warder's desk. In the the first place, if you had done six months or over of your sentence you got your weekly tobacco ration, consisting of half an ounce of coarse navy cut. This tobacco was supposed to last you a week. You were never supplied with cigarettes, which were illegal within the walls of the prison. All cigarettes smoked in prison were hand-rolled out of shredded navy-cut, pieces of sanitary-paper being most commonly used for rolling the tobacco in. The tobacco which you got in your ration on Saturdays, and other tobacco which you managed to get smuggled in, was very precious and took the place of money as prison currency. Tobacco was legal tender up to almost any amount.

In addition to the tobacco, you also received – if your luck was in – a letter from a relative, a sweetheart, a friend, an acquaintance, from somebody in the outside world who had not forgotten you with the years. If your conduct was good you were allowed two letters and two visits of a quarter-of-an-hour each per month. You were allowed to find out whom a letter was from, and then if you didn't want it you could decline it. The same with a visit. But there were, alas, very many convicts (the majority, in fact) who year in, year out, never got a letter or a visit. Such a one would not decline a letter even if it was from a creditor.

Then you went up into the section and found a clean shirt, pair of pants, and night-shirt waiting for you. (Your handkerchief you were supposed to wash yourself.) All this washing was done in the laundry in the women's section. You got your own shirt, night-shirt and pants back from the wash each week: because when you were issued with an article of apparel you took the precaution of sewing your prison number on to it in two or three different places. Nevertheless, there was nearly always trouble about the laundry on a Saturday. Mostly it was your night-shirt that was missing. Because night-shirt material was the best for making tinder out of, and the cleaners up in the section spent part of Saturday morning in burning tinder for the week. It was tough, when you came into your cage and found that there wasn't a night-shirt laid out for you. Because the cleaner would swear that he put that night-shirt there, for you, especially, he remembers; and if you still look doubtful about it he can bring along anyone of half-a-dozen fellow-cleaners, and they will all swear that they also noticed and remembered particularly, that there was a night-shirt put for you there, in your cage, on the floor, right on top of your pants. They remembered because they noticed your number. They wouldn't be so sure about the man in the cage next to you: perhaps he had been given a night-shirt: perhaps he hadn't; they just couldn't be sure. But about your night-shirt they had no doubts. They remembered particularly that it was a blue night-shirt. (In view of the fact that all prison night-shirts are made out of blue jean, it would have been surprising if they had noticed that that night-shirt was not blue.)

Anyway, if one of your garments was missing, things could be made very unpleasant for you. If you had influence with somebody in the store, then some sort of arrangement could usually be made. A convict-storeman could steal a garment for you out of the stock, and then replace it when the next consignment came along. Failing that, you had to report the loss to your section officer, who would record the matter in writing and pass on the note to the head discipline-warder in the hall. Eventually you would be brought before the chief-warder. If you were lucky you would get off with a reprimand and loss of privileges for a month. If your luck was out you went to solitary. A convict was, of course, not mug enough to go on reporting the loss of articles out of his cell: he would report it once but not again.

The food is very good on Saturdays and Sundays. And you spend quite a lot of time out in the yard at the week-end. The

Good Conduct second time (and more) offenders exercise in what is known as the star yard, where there are palms and grass lawns. But no first offender, no matter how good his conduct is, is allowed out of the bleak, stony, sunless passageway that is known, by courtesy-title, as the first offenders' yard.

On Saturday afternoons and Sundays (during the time in which we were not locked up) we used to walk about this yard, or sit in the cement gutter, up against the wall, and talk, or play chess, card games not being allowed. And, of course, we used to read a lot. We could get books sent in from outside, and there was quite a large prison library.

Oh, yes, and another prison institution: the hair-cut. You had to have your hair close-cropped once or twice a month with a number nought clipper, which also served as a razor. You'd be surprised to see how short a number nought hair-clipper, properly sharpened on a piece of flat glass and manipulated by an expert, can crop your beard. A warder would appoint any convict to the job of barber. The man we had as barber in the first offenders' section was doing a term of natural life for murder. He had already been inside about six years, during four of which he had acted as barber. I can only say that he was highly-skilled with the number nought clippers. I feel sure he could have held his own with any of the long-timer barbers in the old offenders' sections.

So much for ordinary days in the week, including Sundays: for I have already mentioned the Sunday church services. But Christmas day is different in prison. (By the way, have you heard this old joke? –

"How long did the judge give you this time?"

"Ten days."

"Gawd, you're lucky, man. Only ten days?"

"Yes, but they're Christmas days.")

Anyway, on Christmas day you get plum-pudding. And you don't work. And the Salvation Army band comes and plays a few hymn-tunes in front of the main-gate about nine o'clock at night. And some of the convicts sing lustily because the warders don't stop you from singing on Christmas. Other convicts, who don't like the Salvation Army, get up on to their stools and shout "Shut up, you b——s!" through the bars of their cells.

This little description covers, however inadequately, the salient features of prison life as it is lived in terms of the regulations.

But irregularities are known to take place, in prison as well as in other places. I shall deal with some of the more outstanding irregularities later.

But about the singing on Christmas days. It has one or two rather human aspects. Convicts are not allowed to sing at work or in the cells or at exercise. They may only sing hymns at the Sunday church services. So they rather let themselves go on Christmas day. (They also hold little sing-songs quite often, in a corner of some yard, at week-ends, but they can't sing very loudly, and a warder comes round at intervals to shut them up.) But on Christmas it's all in. And it's queer to hear some of the songs the old-timers sing. Songs that were popular when they were last at liberty. I thought it was sad that you could work out how long a man had been in prison when you heard him sing. You could work out the number of years by his repertoire. I wonder if it is the same thing with a caged singing bird: if the bird remembers only the notes that he heard in the woodland, long ago and far away.

But there were other songs that you couldn't guess the length of a man's incarceration by. They were the genuine prison songs, which I had never heard before, and which I have never heard since coming out of prison. These songs could never be sung very loudly. About half-a-dozen convicts would gather together, against a wall or in some corner a good distance away from a warder, and they would sing. And because they had to sing softly, their songs had a quality of nostalgic fragrance and honey-suckle wistfulness that they would not have had, if they were roared out throatily from full lungs. The prison songs fascinated me. I felt they could have been composed only in a prison. And I felt that the right place for singing them was within the walls of a prison. Many of them were dagga rookers' songs. There is something about these prison songs that haunts me. They seem to have been composed only for singing softly, five or six men standing in a corner, and one man standing a little distance off to say "Edge that" when a warder comes too near.

Now, I have written more or less everything that happens normally in prison. Stories, boob tales, characters and all the rest I shall deal with later. And if I have succeeded in conveying nothing of the misery of prison existence, the soul-killing monotony, the bleak gloom and brutality, then I am very glad. Because these are things that nobody should pen. For one thing, you can't. You only make a fool of yourself if you try.

If at any time I say something in these pages that makes prison seem an unpleasant place to be in, it is only because that happens to be incidental to the narrative, at some stage or other.

I would be acting falsely if I gave the impression that prison life is something unalleviated in its despair. I did not find it so.

On the other hand, it would be equally untrue if I tried to pretend that the reality of being in prison falls in any way short of the ideas one has about it before making acquaintance with a gaol in the capacity of a convict. Nobody who has been in prison would ever want to go back again. And to me the thought of being locked up again, even for one night, even on a charge like being drunk and disorderly – when I know I can pay a pound fine in the morning – the very thought of it appals me.

Chapter 4

I WORKED IN the printers' shop for about a year. The head-warder in the printers, having begun, as I have said, by rating my intelligence as higher than that of the average convict (for which reason he had started off by putting me in charge of the paper-store) ended up by assessing my intelligence as a good deal lower than that of the average convict. At all events, when I fell in for work again, in the printers' span, one morning, I was informed that I had been given a change of labour.

"What span, sir?" I asked of the head-warder who imparted this information to me.

"Ye're on the stone-pile," the head-warder announced, contempt in his voice, and turned on his heel.

The news came as a bit of a shock to me. For I believed that I had been making fair to middling progress at type-setting. I knew I couldn't set a stick of type as quickly as a man who had been doing that sort of work for years. But I also prided myself on the belief (quite erroneous, no doubt), that even if I wasn't too quick at it I could nevertheless set quite clean. The head-warder turned on his heel, and so I shuffled off, also, without any more speech, down the rows of convicts, to a large gang of prisoners whose trousers and jackets were red with the soil from the excavation pits, and whose hats were crumpled from being exposed to rain and weather, and whose boots were clogged with dried clay. They were a pretty villainous-looking mob, the stone-yard span. Even in prison, among the spans working in the other shops, they stood out in point of appearance: their foreheads were lower; their jaws were more stubbly and seemed to stick out more; they seemed more un-prepossessing and more hulking and more brutalised and more lost, too, somehow, than any other group of men in that prison. (And when you see a whole lot of convicts together, you don't get the impression of being confronted by a mob of Adonises.)

Because he is, in the first place, abnormal, the average convict is less good-looking than the average healthy-minded citizen who is too clever to manifest his criminal tendencies to the point where he gets landed behind bars. Then, you've just got to think how a convict is dressed. Those battered, shapeless boots; those ridiculous knee-breeches surmounting legs en-cased in black stockings variegated with horizontal red stripes; and that washed-out brown jacket that hangs like a sack on you; and that comical-looking white canvas ticket-pocket, hanging on your chest like a burlesque decoration; and as likely as not you are wearing your red-spotted handkerchief knotted around your throat; and your towel: oh, I have for-gotten to mention that funny white linen towel: it is easy to realise why I had forgotten about that apology for a towel until this moment: you are not allowed to leave your towel in your cell, because it gets grabbed and burned as tinder: so they have got this regulation that you have got to carry your towel on your person all the time: you have got to carry it folded, *with part of it tucked into your breeches at the back, the other part to hang out three inches below your jacket:* that is why I had forgotten about the towel until this moment: how can you remember something that you don't see, because it hangs out from the back of your breeches, underneath your jacket? But you see the other man's towel, of course – whenever he turns his back on you.

So there you are. In addition to all his other sartorial dis-abilities, the hundred per cent, classic-model convict also walks about with a piece of folded linen towel hanging out behind his backside, like the end of a shirt that he has forgotten to tuck in. Add to all the foregoing the fact that his head is cropped short and that his face is covered in black stubble and that his body and clothes are alike impregnated with a peculiar kind of stink – the characteristic prison odour, a stink of misery and male faeces, you begin to think after you have been in prison for a lot of years – and you realise that a group of convicts constitutes a somewhat uninspiring sight. But when I lined up with the stone-yard gang, that morning after I had been sacked from the printers, I felt that the convicts who had been my work-mates until now looked like South African ambassadors at foreign courts compared with the debased and brutalised thugs and scoundrels and cut-throats and yeggmen among whom my lot was now cast.

I went up to the head-warder in charge of the stone-breakers and gave him my ticket.

"Fall in," he said, and his voice held a marked lack of enthusiasm.

I felt crushed. Working in the stone-yard was regarded as the lowest job in prison. The off-scourings of the gaol were dumped into the stone-yard. It was even better to be in the refuse-span, they said. Because if you were in the refuse-span you could sometimes pick up a slice of bread and butter on the floor of one of the warders' lavatories. I felt very sad that morning. I had been chucked on to the stone-pile. I was one of a lot of human derelicts who looked at me with suspicion mingled with contempt. They despised themselves because their own capabilities, and in a prison of all places, had been rated so low that the authorities could class them only as unskilled labourers, as fit only for the heaviest and most soulless form of drudgery. And as is always the case with the outcast, because he despises himself for being outside the social pale, he has the most unspeakable contempt for any other human being in a like case with himself. I felt that the whole stone-yard gang that morning was a curled sneer. Every convict in that span despised me because I had also been relegated to the stone-pile. I had also been flung in with the off-scourings of the Swartklei Great Prison.

"Forward!" the discipline head-warder shouted. The stone-pile span shuffled off to their place of work. And from force of habit I again made the sign of the cross, religiously, when our gang marched through the mortuary gate.

2

That year in the printers hadn't been so bad, I reflected, seated on the stone-pile. I had got to learn the ropes. A blue-coat had taken a fancy to me. I saw him only rarely – on Sundays, mostly, at church service. He was locked up in penal. So he couldn't go out to work in one of the shops for another year or so, since the first part of a blue-coat's sentence has to be spent in penal. But he was entitled to buy groceries every month. Every convict receives a gratuity of threepence per working day: between six and seven shillings per month. Out of this money, after he has been in prison a year or so, depending on the length of his sentence, he is allowed to spend three shillings and six-pence per month on approved groceries. Now, I was twenty-one years of age, healthy and with a healthy appetite, and I was not yet allowed to supplement the prison rations with the monthly order for groceries, to be paid for out of my gratuity.

I didn't get enough to eat, really. At all events, I was hungry nearly all the time. There was nothing wrong with that, of course. I think it is a very good thing for you not to be allowed to over-eat at any time, particularly not in your early manhood. But this blue-coat, who was about thirty-five years of age and whose name was Pym, was entitled to groceries. The first I knew of his existence was when a cleaner one afternoon when I was coming back from work met me at the foot of the stairs leading to A2 Section and slipped a note and a small packet of sweets into my hand.

"It's from Pym," the cleaner said, winking, and disappeared.

After I was locked up in my cage I opened the packet of sweets and the note about the same time. But I was more interested in the contents of the brown-paper package than I was in the contents of the note. Anyway, from the way Pym wrote, it appeared that he had fallen in love with me. He had seen me march out, morning after morning, on the way to the workshops, and he had stood on the stool in front of the barred window of his cell, and had watched me every day – four times a day, and he had now made bold to write to me enclosing some sweets and inviting me to meet him at the Wesleyan service on Sunday. I went and met him. More notes and groceries followed. Eventually he used to send me all his groceries every month: butter, curry-powder, condensed milk, cheese – things like that. I didn't like his company very much. But the groceries were useful. And he asked nothing more of me than that I should come and sit next to him on a bench during the Wesleyan service, every Sunday, and sing out of the same hymn-book with him. And he wrote me letters very regularly, sent by the hand of the same cleaner who always winked when he said, "It's from Pym." The letters contained all sorts of endearments, but they made no suggestions about sodomy. I was puzzled how to reply to them. He also sent me scraps of tobacco at first, saved out of his own ration.

But I shortly afterwards got into the way of having tobacco

smuggled in to me. The smuggling would work this way: a friend of the convict's would send five pounds to an address where the warder would collect the money and keep half for himself. For the two-ten the warder bought navy-cut tobacco which he would smuggle into the prison in quantities of a few tins at a time. The warder would hand the tobacco to the "channel" – some long-timer with lots of previous convictions who had probably spent years in getting the warder to the stage where he trusted him. This convict would again take half the tobacco for himself and pass on the remainder to some other convict, who would also help himself out of the "poke", as they called it. The tobacco would frequently pass through five or six hands before it reached the convict whose friend or relative had sent the money to the warder. When I first started off getting in tobacco "under the lap," I must have been pretty far down in the scale. There must have been quite a long chain of hands through which the tobacco passed – each man helping himself out of the parcel for his trouble – before what was left of it eventually came to me. Because I wouldn't get very much tobacco for my five pounds. But with the years, through more and more intermediaries dropping out, the parcels I got increased in size. Each person who got the tobacco knew only the man immediately before him. I knew only the cleaner who finally handed me the tobacco. Whom he got it from I wouldn't know. And I never knew who the warder was, of course.

It was pretty well-known (or at least suspected) who the warders were who "lumbered". But there was no way of telling which individual warder dealt with any particular convict. And during all the time I was in the Swartklei Great Prison no warder was ever convicted of smuggling. Of all those dozens of warders who could have been given away by the convicts through whom they dealt, during the years I was in prison, not one was ever squealed on. Supposing Warder X was a lumberer. He would deal only through his one prisoner contact. It would be a business that lasted as long as that convict was in prison. And if some other convict went up to that warder and suggested that he should smuggle in tobacco for him, the chances were that the warder would take that convict in front of the Governor and charge him with attempting to suborn him to commit an offence. The convict could get up to three months for that. In that way the warder protected himself. He would get the reputation, officially, that he was a man who could not be tampered with. Unofficially everybody, including the Governor, knew that that warder lumbered.

I don't know what the warder used to do with the money that I got people outside to send him. But I know what I did with the tobacco. I smoked part of it. I had learnt to smoke in prison. Before that I was a non-smoker. Tobacco was money, in prison. And I spent a good deal of my tobacco on food. A half-ounce ration of tobacco was divided into twenty "doppies", each about the size of a smoke. And for five doppies I could get a small tin of hard fat smuggled in to me from the kitchen. (All purchases and barter in prison were illegal. All these transactions had to be carried on sub rosa.) I would melt this fat into my mealie-pap. Or for ten doppies I could buy – again from somebody in the kitchen – a slice of beef and a raw onion. Sometimes, also for about half-a-ration, I would get a pannikin of milk sneaked into my cage in A2 Section from one of the hospital wards. And so on. A convict who smoked heavily would also sell the whole of his monthly three shillings worth of groceries (purchased out of his gratuity money) for a couple of tins of navy-cut.

I would buy an occasional newspaper, not more than three days old, for a couple of doppies. I would bribe one of the library assistants with tobacco to get me an extra book. I would pay the stores-hand something for a better pair of breeches, or for a pair of stockings specially woven in such a way that the horizontal red stripes did not show up very vividly. I would give somebody in the book-binders a ration of tobacco to make me a little note-book that I could write in. And so on. One winter, for two tins of tobacco, I even bought an extra blanket which I used for six weeks, until the section-warder discovered it. The blanket was confiscated and I got six days' solitary confinement on spare diet.

The result was that I no longer required Pym's groceries. Even without the privilege of buying groceries (which I would not be granted for about another year) I was better off than he was, because of what I could buy with smuggled tobacco. I never felt really very friendly towards Pym. But I was sorry for him. I felt sorry for him because he was doing his second blue-coat, and because I felt it must be terrible in penal, and because he had a look of haunted loneliness that was conspicuous even in prison, where most convicts have an expression of closed-in solitariness in their eyes. So for a long time – in fact, until he came out of penal and went to work in one of the shops – I used to go, regularly every Sunday, to sit beside Pym in the Wesleyan church service. The fact that I knew, from his letters, that he must be homosexual, distressed me but did not repel me.

Only after he was released from penal and was allowed to join a workshop span, thereby being enabled to make more frequent contact with me, did Pym start giving me trouble.

3

In the printers there had been a tall, dark convict, handsome in a sort of a backveld way, with whom I had been friendly.

77

His name was Huysmans. He had been a school-teacher on the platteland. He was serving a second sentence for the same kind of offence, that of tampering with little girls. He had only about six more months of his sentence to go when I was sent to work in the printers. On the morning of his discharge I was pleased, of course, for his sake, to see Huysmans get out. But I felt lonely without him, for a good while, in the workshop and in the exercise yard.

It gets awful, after a bit, being locked up in a prison and not seeing a woman. Not hearing a woman's laughter. Having no contact with a woman except when some woman outside writes to you. And you carry that letter inside your shirt until it gets black with grime. And you lie back every night on your blankets and read that letter before the lights go out. And the woman who wrote that letter to you, even if she is a comparative stranger who is merely giving you some news, becomes for you the symbol of all womanhood. And then if you have a snapshot of a woman, of a real woman, of somebody you know (and not just a picture of a woman in an illustrated book, although that is also all right) it is easily the most prized possession any man can boast of in prison. Male and female. It maddens you. Once when my breeches came back from the laundry (in the woman's section of the prison) there was a long dark hair attached to the material. A woman's hair. It could be nothing less. I tried to picture how she looked. I kept that long black hair for years, of course, in the soiled envelope in which I kept a snapshot.

A lot of the talk in a prison is about women. Naturally. And because Huysmans had been convicted of sex-offences, he knew a lot of things from actual experience which I until then had only heard about, and which in the long hours of the night I would brood upon. Men talked of the women they had slept with. And night after night, in the darkness of the cage, I would lie back in misery at the thought that I had listened to all the rubbish about sex being the unforgivable sin, and that for that reason, now that I was locked up in prison without any hopes of as much as seeing a woman again for many years, I had so little with which to console myself.

Through Huysmans's conversation I was able to obtain quite a lot of vicarious thrills.

"Give me a little girl of twelve," Huysmans would say.

Yes, that's fine, I would think. Give me one, also.

"Give me a little girl of twelve," Huysmans would continue, "I nearly got lashes for it, once – the last time I was in, in fact. She was a little girl in standard five. It's lovely flesh at that age, lamb's meat. Her face was rather fat, and she had a cross sort of expression when she was working at the desk or just sitting doing nothing. But she was very pretty when she smiled. One of her front teeth was missing. She also had a couple of freckles on her nose, I remember. But she had full red lips, and when she ran about, playing on the school-ground, her fair hair would blow over her eyes and some strands would also fall down across her red lips. She was shortish and rather plump. And I fell in love with her right away. I used to lean over my desk and watch her going down the road every afternoon, after school. I pretended to be working. But I was all the time watching her. I watched her walking up the road and I got the most passionate feelings at the way she moved her sturdy little haunches. And at the way her short gym-frock fluttered about her thighs.

"But it was easy in the end, man," Huysmans went on, "You got no idea how easy. Only, I got warned for lashes. And my whole career with the Education Department went to hell. Not that that mattered, really. For I found I could do better selling insurance. And then you're your own boss, also. But it's a temptation to me, when I go out selling insurance on the farms. Almost as much temptation as when I was still teaching. That's how they got me on the charge for which I am doing time now. I don't know why it is, but if I go to a farm-house, where there are three daughters, aged respectively twenty-five, eighteen and twelve, I'll always fall for the one aged twelve. And I am a man of thirty-eight.

"But that girl you were talking about," I reminded Huysmans, asking the question as unconcernedly as possible, afraid I might be sounding too eager, "That school-girl that you said – that you said was quite easy?"

I was hoping that Huysmans would tell me exactly how easy, with details if possible. He did.

"I just kept her in after school, one day," Huysmans announced, "And after all the children had gone, as far as I could judge, I asked this girl, Tossie her name was, to come up to my table. She put her hand on the side of the table. I was sitting on the chair. The next thing we both knew was that I put my hand over hers. I was afraid to talk, in case she could tell by my voice how excited I was. I couldn't find my breath. And then I looked up at her again. And I saw her bosom. It moved up and down, fluttering with the way her heart was beating. Her breasts were well-developed for her age. I could see, through her dress, by her agitation that she was responding to the feelings inside me that were making my knees tremble –"

And so Huysmans related, in juicy detail, the story of his seduction of Tossie, and of his subsequent life of immorality with her, which lasted for three months, and would have gone on longer, he said, if her father had not made Tossie go and give evidence against him. If it hadn't been for her father,

Huysmans declared, the charge against him could still have been withdrawn.

"What the jury really found me guilty on," Huysmans explained, "was the packet of sweets the detective found under my pillow. I had got Tossie to agree to say that she had spent the night with her auntie, again. But her elder sister said she hadn't. And so the next thing was her father got the story out of her with a sjambok. And the shop-keeper said he had remembered selling me that packet of sweets earlier in the afternoon. As though one packet of sweets isn't just like another. But it was a wonderful time while it lasted."

Huysmans went on to say that even nowadays, sometimes when his cell-mates (Huysmans was not a first offender, and consequently slept in a community-cell) were asleep, and he was lying thinking of the past, then he would remember those three months in which he had lived with Tossie at regular intervals.

It gave him the most wonderful sensations, he said . . .

It was all right for Huysmans, I would reflect bitterly. For him those experiences with Tossie had been a living reality. For me – I had to console myself with a tale that had been told. In the hush of the night I would have to imagine myself in the role of Huysmans, Tossie's seducer. I would have to think what she was like, first. I made her out of synthetic pieces of girls whose appearance I could still vaguely remember. To this image I added the more vivid details from Huysmans's descriptive passages. There she was, Tossie. I had manufactured an image of her for myself. I had made her so that I could get the same thrills out of thinking of Tossie as I imagined her to be, as Huysmans got out of recalling the girl that he had known in the flesh. I gave her wide blue eyes; and her knees were slightly roughened; and her lips glowed red; and I knew all of her body.

In my imaginings I put myself in Huysmans's place, there in that little class-room, with the sun coming in slant-wise at the window to fall on Tossie's upraised skirt. And those soft, creamy hollows under her wayward breasts. Lord, I knew Tossie much better than Huysmans did.

"That was a wonderful time, those three months," Huysmans said, "Even though I nearly got lashes for it. There is nothing in the world as lovely as tender young lamb's meat, like what Tossie has got."

"Yes," I answered, nodding solemnly, "Like what Tossie has got."

4

The funny part of working in the stone-yard, after I had got over the humiliation of my demotion, was that I liked it. I had read somewhere something a man had written about a galley-slave, who, looking back on the years in which he had been chained to the oar, said that he had at least served his time with men. And that was what I was beginning to feel about the stone-pile. I felt that whatever we were, we, the offscourings of a large prison, whatever else we were, we were men. I was serving my time with men, even though not one of us was much of a man.

The work in the stone-yard is very simple. It's merely a matter of sitting on the ground, with a hammer in your hand, making big stones smaller. And how you can think, sitting out there in the angle of the wall, convicts on all sides of you, row upon endless row of them, and the sun shines flat down on your head on a fine day, and the water flows down into your neck when it rains. After a while I began to feel that this was a perfect life. After I had got used to having my breeches caked in clay all day. And my palms calloused from the hammer, and

82

engrained with dust. And my boots shapeless and bemired. I wouldn't exchange that job for any other in the boob. I could sit there by the hour, talking to the man next to me, if the mood took me, remaining silent in my own thoughts if I felt that way. All the warders were concerned about was that you should keep the hammer going at a reasonably quick pace. And they didn't mind if you talked to the man beside you either, as long as you didn't raise your voice much, and you spoke out of the side of your mouth. I felt that just in being allowed to sit under the sky you were accorded the highest privilege the prison had to offer you. They had given me a good job, and they didn't know it! And it was a job that I needn't be afraid of losing . . .

Afterwards they started extending the prison wall. That was our job. Those of us who were physically fit were divided up into groups. We excavated a big piece of mountain-side; we built a length of rail-track for moving coco-pans along; we got a crane delivered and we transported tremendous rocks on it; one day the load we put on was too heavy (for what did we know about cranes anyway?) and so the jib broke, part of it crashing on to the head of a convict underneath, killing him on the spot; it gave me a queer sensation when I helped to wash his brains off the crane; we carried hundreds of sacks of cement on our backs, from the front gate where the stuff got delivered to where the coco-pan track started; we moved thousands of tons of earth and stone by wheel-barrow and by hand and by coco-pan; and we built a high wall right into the middle of a koppie, making room for another vast area of workshops, and we took a certain modified pride, we of the stone-yard, in the thought that nobody would be able to climb over that wall and make his escape from the prison, unless he had ladders and all sorts of other equipment. No convict was going to climb out too easy over the wall we had built.

I once spoke to a blue-coat who was on the point of going out. He had served nine years of his indeterminate sentence, and the Prison Board had recommended him for discharge. In a few days' time he would be released. He would walk out of the front gate a free man.

"What are you going to do when you get out?" I asked this blue-coat.

He told me.

"I got about twenty pounds saved up in gratuity," he answered, "And I'm going to rent a room in Vrededorp. I'm going to pay the rent slap down in advance for a month. And I'm going to buy enough sherry to last me for a month. And enough boom to last me for a month. And I'm going to hire a kafir. And I'm going to have enough money left to pay him in advance for a month. And what this kafir has got to do is he has to come and wake me up six o'clock every morning, and he has got to say, 'The section-warder wants you,' and I'll answer – regular like that every morning – 'To hell with the section-warder,' and I'll turn round and go back to sleep again."

That was his idea of paradise. My own dreams of bliss centred around having a girl like Tossie.

Chapter 5

A QUEER THING that I found among first-offender convicts – and something that I thought very much to their credit – was the fact that they were all of them innocent. Every man Jack of them. And without exception – bar one. Of all the convicts doing stretches in A2 Section (the section occupied by the first-offenders) I was the only one who was guilty. Among the old offenders there was also a pretty substantial proportion that was innocent (or that had been framed), but the percentage of innocent men was not nearly so high as among the first offenders. For that reason I respected the first offenders. But I felt very dismal there, all the same, as the one guilty man chucked in with a whole lot of innocent lambs, and guileless simpletons who were only trying to do somebody else a favour, and angels with large, white wings, and plaster saints . . .

You have no idea what a source of distress this was to me. It gave me the most awful feeling of inferiority, after a while.

I would talk to a man in the first offenders' section. A stranger to me. But rather decent-looking, somehow. I would go up to him on exercise, let us say, and I would introduce myself, and I would say that I am in for murder, and I am doing ten years. How long are you doing, and what for?

And he would always begin his answer with the remark, "Well, of course, I didn't do it, but the judge gave me five years for arson." Or he would say, "I know nothing about it, but the prosecution claimed that I raped a kafir-girl, which is so blasted silly when you think that the only evidence they had was a piece of her bloomers lying in my back-yard. Who has ever heard of a kafir-girl wearing red-flannel bloomers in January?" Or he would say, "I got two years for taking a cheque along to the bank, man, a cheque that I received in all good faith. It was only a cheque for nine thousand four hundred pounds. Imagine a man in my position doing anything so silly, and just for nine thousand four hundred pounds. Why, my good name alone is worth much more than that."

"Was," I would say. Or something to that effect.

"What do you mean, 'was'?" he would ask.

"Well, your good name isn't worth that amount any more, is it?" I would remark.

But you have got no idea how inferior I felt. Every man in the first offenders' section I spoke to was innocent. And he would explain his innocence to me in such detail, and his countenance, as he spoke, would be lit up with so pure a radiance, so noble a refulgence, that I believed him implicitly, and I felt very sorry for him, and I wondered how he could bring himself, from the noble elevation of his guiltlessness, to hold converse with so sorry a worm as myself – I wondered how he could even talk with this shabby felon shuffling along by his side. And I would walk beside my new acquaintance, my shoulders drooping and my self-esteem in the dust, pondering on how lost a part of creation I must be. I was a member of some sub-pariah species. I was in prison, and, on top of everything else, guilty.

I got so, in time, whenever I went up to a man in the first-offenders' section, and I hadn't spoken to him before, because there were so many first offenders, or because he had only just arrived, that I would approach him, very diffidently, and I would say, "Look here, old fellow, I know you didn't do it, but what are you in for?" Or I would say, "I know you're inno-

86

cent, mate. I can see it all over you. But how long did they frame you for?" And then they would tell me everything, about how they tried to save the family honour, or about how the johns rung a dirty on them with fabricated evidence, and I would feel very low and evil-smelling. And afterwards, when the man I was talking to would say to me, "And what is your name? And you, too, are, of course, innocent?" then I would look down at the ground very shame-facedly, and I would say, no, I wasn't really innocent, and that I was in fact doing time because I had been justly convicted. I could see then how hard it was for the man I was talking to to keep on remaining in my company, and that my very presence seemed to make him shudder. Since I was the only one there, in the whole of the first offenders' section, who didn't claim to be innocent, I was shunned on all sides.

It was worst on those days when a new batch of convicts arrived in A2 section from Cape Town, or some such place. Especially if it was a rather large escort that arrived at night, and one or two of them got accommodation in cages near where I was penned. Then it was terrible. They would go on talking right through the night. The night-warder would come round periodically and tell them to shut up, or he would charge them; and they would remain quiet for a little while; but afterwards they would get going again, and they would keep it up until the early hours of the morning. And each one of these new arrivals, each person who had come up in this latest escort, would insist on talking about how badly he had been treated. He would sling off at the john who had pinched him, and he would call this john all the mongrels in the world. And then he would say that the Judge was deaf and in his second child-hood and corrupt; and that the Crown Prosecutor was a ——house of the first water; and that his own Counsel was the

87

most depraved of the whole lot. "Anybody would think that the police didn't have enough lies against me, without my own Counsel also wanting to give them a hand. If it wasn't for my advocate, I'd be a free man to-day," he would say.

They would go on like that far into the night, these new arrivals. Sometimes, when I was very unlucky, it would happen that the section-warder would put two new convicts on either side of me. And then they would lie there talking to each other, oor en weer across my cage, and I would go almost frantic at all the drivel they talked. And I didn't have any sort of redress. How could I request innocent men to stop discussing the injustice that had been visited on them, when I myself was as guilty as hell?

And these first-offender convicts would come along and squeal to me. I would have to listen to five or six different kinds of bleat every time I strolled about the first-offender exercise yard at a week-end. There was a lofty kind of condescension about the way they addressed me. But they seemed to feel better for having explained to a third party just how the mis-carriage of justice had come about that had landed them behind the bars. There was one man, I remember, who had also been in the condemned cell for murder – a couple of years before me – and who had also been reprieved. And he didn't believe that his sentence had been commuted because the higher authorities had taken compassion on him – as I believed in respect of my own case. Oh, no, it was different with him. He was reprieved because no matter what lies the prosecution told about him, he had a clear conscience all the time, and the truth was great and it would prevail. The truth would prevail to such an extent, even, he declared, that one of these days he would be released from prison through a special discharge and the law would find out how grievously he had been wronged and he would receive many thousands of pounds in compensation.

"It's terrible here, inside this boob," this man said to me, "I am even beginning to talk prison slang like the most hardened of the old offenders. Did you hear me say 'boob?' And the food. Hell, you got no idea how bad the food is here in this section. On a farm we wouldn't feed pigs on food like this. And how the hell can I keep working all morning in the tailors' shop at that blessed machine, just on one ladle of mealie-pap? You don't know how much I have already suffered, and how much I am still going through. At this very moment I am suffering from living under these conditions. It's all right for you, of course. I can understand that you don't squeal. You see, you're guilty. You're in a different boat from us chaps that's innocent. So you're all right. You're blasted lucky you didn't get the rope. From what I know of your case (I am not judging you now, mind: each person knows best what is going on in the secret recesses of his own heart) but from what I have heard of your case, if I had been the Minister of Justice, or the Governor-General in Council, I don't think I would have reprieved you. In fact, I'm blasted certain I wouldn't have reprieved you. Now you know the truth. That's exactly how I feel about you. I always believe that it's best to be straight with people. Even if the truth hurts."

And then I would say no, it was quite all right. I could understand how he must feel about me. But I couldn't help being in that prison, along with him. It looked like the law sometimes nodded, and so by mistake put guilty people in prison as well, and that made it very unpleasant for the others.

"I have said just that same thing often myself," this man replied, "There ought to be a separate kind of prison for us chaps that's innocent. If we get mixed up with your kind of person we'll just go from bad to worse. They say you smoke dagga. Is that right?"

"Well, I do have a pull now and again," I admitted, "When I have it offered me."

"And they say that you got chucked out of the printers' shop right into the stone yard," he continued, "for smoking dagga behind the cropper. Behind which cropper was it?"

"That big one next to the cylinder," I explained, "We had put a big piece of cardboard alongside the machine, and we were smoking dagga there. But the smoke rose up above the card-board, and the screw sniffed it. But I wasn't the only one he caught there. And then he didn't catch any of us, really. He couldn't prove it was dagga, or that we were smoking at all. So he never laid a charge against us. Baldy Jones chewed up the dagga stoppie. He chewed it all up. I admire him for that. He didn't spit out even a bit of the brown paper. But he was blue for a week after that. All the same that wasn't the reason the head warder chucked me out of his shop. Because there were five of us behind the machine. Why should he have picked on me? And, in any case, he was never able to prove a thing."

"And they also say you're a sodomite," this first offender who had been wrongfully convicted went on, seeming to swell with the pure pride of innocence as he spoke, "They say you are some blue-coat's rabbit."

"No," I replied, "That isn't so. Blue-coat Pym, who is still in penal, sent me a few packets of sweets, and afterwards he used to give me groceries. But he doesn't any more. I have found a channel and I get tobacco sent in to me regularly. So Pym doesn't need to give me groceries any more. I get more than he does. But he still writes me notes, now and again."

"What's in them?"

"Oh, you know, just soft stuff. Slobber and all that. How lonely he is in his peter –"

"There you are, you see? You can't stop talking that awful boob slang. What more does he say in his notes?"

"Oh, well, just about how good-looking he thinks I am, and how his seeing me going to and from work every day and meeting me in chapel on Sundays are the only things that cheer him up. And he also says he wants me to come and sleep with him."

This last bit was fictitious. I just made it up to annoy this old whited sepulchre. I wanted to give him an excuse for some more Pharisaism.

"Sleep with you, hey?" he snorted, "I got a good mind to report that to the Governor. But it just shows you what I've been saying. It's not right to put the innocent into the same prison with the guilty. You can't have the sheep in with the goats. You can't make fish of one and flesh of another. That's how you behave here in prison, instead of trying to be an example to some of these incorrigible criminals. If the higher authorities knew the stamp of person you are, I'm blasted sure they would have thought twice about reprieving you. What more does that blue-coat write to you in those notes?"

As I have indicated, it was hard for me, in the first offenders' section, since I was regarded with contumely all the time by a lot of innocent men.

2

As I have said, I spent about six months of my time in the stone-yard, sitting down chopping stones. Then they started on the large-scale excavation of the side of the koppie, and the work became more interesting. But with all this new activity of moving part of a mountain with a crane and coco-pans and wheel-barrows, and all this dressing stones and mixing mortar for that long, towering wall – as a result of all this fevered rushing around there began to develop a certain measure of friction as between warder and convict and between convict and convict which was not there in those placid days when we were only making largish stones smaller and had not embarked on this ambitious construction project. The warders wanted more work out of the convicts, and more efficient work. The convicts were sullen in their response, and visited their ill-humour on each other.

"What you want is my boot up your backside again," a warder would shout at a young convict, "But you're used to having other things up your backside. That's why you can't work during the day. Too many blue-coats –"

Or he would shout, "Swing that —— pick higher. Put some more blasted guts into it. If I catch you loafing again I'll report you to the Governor, you blasted, motherless, cock-eyed sod." This addressed to some other convict, and so it would go on.

There was a convict in the stone-yard that they called Slangvel. He got his nickname from the bluish appearance of his skin, a sort of slaty mottle. From deeply ingrained grime, I suppose. He had a powerful physique, with enormous shoulders and a thick, bull neck. He washed once a month. I was always interested in Slangvel's ablutions. For some obscure reason he would never wash in the section. But once a month, in the afternoon, a few minutes before the fall-in signal, when we were allowed to relax for a little on smoking days, Slangvel would go to the tap with a bucket and a piece of soap. He would fill the bucket at the tap and walk some distance away and sit on a pile of bricks, with the bucket in front of him, and he would start washing. The first thing he did, always, was to take off his boots and stockings. Incredible quantities of filth were revealed when he peeled off his stockings. Then he put his feet in the bucket. In no time the water would be black with dirt and greasy with floating slime. Then he would take out his feet, dry them on the towel hanging from the back of his breeches, and start washing his hands. When this operation was completed he would kneel down in front of the bucket and in the filthy, black, greasy, soapy, stinking water . . . he would proceed to wash his face.

At various times some of the other convicts spoke to Slangvel about this singular procedure, explaining that if he washed his face first it would be in clean water. They said he should reverse the operational order of his ablutions. But Slangvel could never see the point. "I wash," he said, "And when I'm clean I'm clean."

Slangvel was a man of few words, and those few were uttered in a low sort of growl. He was a heavy dagga-rooker. He resented the new activities connected with the extension of the prison-wall. He very much preferred the old days, when he could sit down all day long, after a boom-rook, and just allow his hammer to fall up and down, and he didn't have to think and he didn't have to talk.

There was a saw-mill on the edge of the stone-yard. About a dozen convicts worked there under the supervision of a warder. They sawed up tree trunks for the carpenters' shop and they also sawed up the bones from the bone-yard. One day a convict sawed up his hand. Two fingers were severed completely. This caused a bit of excitement. The convict was in a bad way. He collapsed into the saw-dust in front of the machine and the warder ordered a couple of the convicts to pick him up and carry him through to the hospital. They had to go through the mortuary-gate. I have explained that the rules lay it down

93

that every convict passing through from the workshops into the section has got to be searched. The warder on duty at the mortuary-gate that day was a middle-aged man who was said to be somewhat unfeeling in his attitude towards the convicts, who nicknamed him Billy the Bastard.

The little procession approached the mortuary-gate: a couple of convicts carrying the injured man between them, and a discipline warder walking a few paces behind. Billy the Bastard halted them. The discipline warder explained what had happened. The man was unconscious; half his hand had been sawn away; he was bleeding profusely. They had to hurry, the discipline warder said.

"You know the regulations," Billy the Bastard replied, imperturbably, "And I got to carry out me orders. I can't let any convict through from the workshops without I search him."

So he made the two convicts lay the unconscious man down on the ground and he proceeded to search them methodically. After that he stooped down and ran his fingers up and down the bloody form of the unconscious convict who had had his hand mangled. Then he said, all right, they could pass through.

Afterwards, when another warder mentioned the matter to Billy the Bastard, and enquired from him, by way of conversation, as to why he had thought it necessary to search the unconscious man as well, he was overheard to answer, "How do I know he didn't have dagga on him? For all I knew the whole thing could have been a lurk to lumber dagga into the hospital. Where would I be then?"

The sequel to that little incident was rather funny. The accident at the saw-mill occurred in the early part of the day on which Slangvel indulged in his monthly wash. Slangvel took up the bucket and went up to the tap. He was very blue with dagga. He had been smoking it all day, they found out after-

94

wards. And so it was with the most beatific visions swimming before his eyes that he came to the tap. He was in a lovely world of bright-hued unreality. At that moment a convict at the saw-mill discovered, in the saw-dust, a bloody piece of finger that had come off the injured man's hand earlier in the day. The convict picked up the finger. Then he spotted Slangvel at the tap. He decided to pull his leg. He guessed Slangvel would be blue, but he didn't know how blue. He walked up to Slangvel, who had just started to fill his pail.

The convict held up his hand. Between his own fingers he grasped the bloody stump he had picked up out of the sawdust.

"Look, Slangvel," the convict exclaimed, "I got six fingers. Look, you can count them. Six fingers!"

Out of that gaudy paradise into which the blue smoke of the dagga had taken him, out of that slow, sensuous world of silken movements and voluptuous women, Slangvel was suddenly transported, by the convict's shout, into a sort of in-between region that he didn't know at all well. He looked at the convict's hand. He blinked. Those fingers. Six. And one of them loose. Yes. One finger loose from the others. Slangvel looked again. Yes, he hadn't been mistaken. What he had seen, at the start, was right. It wasn't just a dagga hallucination. That convict there really was holding up – really was holding up –

Slangvel moaned. It was too much for him. His mind, not too bright at the best of times, couldn't cope with this at all. Slangvel moaned again, a long slow moan, and then he dropped the bucket and subsided forward into the concrete gutter in front of the tap. In falling he struck his chin against the edge of the concrete. He was out for the count. The dagga, and the shock about that finger, and his violent contact with the concrete – these were too much for him. Slangvel lay unconscious beside the tap, which was still running: some of the water ran over him without reviving him: there was a deep gash in his chin.

So there was another convict ready for hospital.

This time it was a stone-yard detail that carried an unconscious convict through the mortuary-gate into the hospital. For the second time that day Billy the Bastard was confronted with an unconscious convict, with blood running from him, being carried through the mortuary-gate. It was pretty tough going: convicts were fainting all over the place like ducks on a hot day on the farm.

The discipline-warder argued, but Billy the Bastard was adamant. The convicts had to be searched. So Slangvel was put down on the ground in front of the mortuary-gate. And this time Billy the Bastard's luck was dead in. He said he had to search the convicts for dagga . . .

He found enough dagga on Slangvel to render a whole city unconscious.

3

One day, while we were still sitting peacefully with our stone-hammers, in calm convict-rows, before we had started extending the wall, a blue-coat, Texas Fraser, told me a little story about a woman he loved. I was really moved by this tale. Tex Fraser was doing his second blue-coat. He was a tall, thin man, very emaciated looking. His face was seamed with deep wrinkles. And he was toothless. When he smiled he displayed two rows of empty gums. And yet, when he spoke, there were times when I could picture Tex Fraser as he had been in the old days, before he had done his first coat. He must have looked quite the lad, then, I should imagine, with his shoulders set up very straight and tall, and a devil-may-care look in his eyes.

(It is singular how in books novelists romanticise this devil-may-care look, and how in real life girls fall for it. But it is only a criminal look. Every criminal has got it, until he starts off on his first blue-coat.)

The story Blue-Coat Tex Fraser told me, one afternoon when we were seated side by side in front of a pile of stones, and the warder was yawning in the sunlight, affected me a good deal during the telling. But afterwards I started getting doubts about it.

"That was Maggie Jones," Tex Fraser said, talking sideways so that the warder couldn't see too clearly that he was talking, "I dunno how I come to fall for her. She was a damn nice bit of skirt. The best-looking moll I'd set eyes on in years. She was dark and her face was long and thin, but smiley, if you know what I means, and her hips was broad. Well, I was working the hug in them days, and I was doing good."

"What is the hug, Tex?" I asked, also trying to talk sideways, so the screw wouldn't jerry to me talking.

I felt, somehow, that when Tex Fraser said he was "doing good," it didn't mean that he was going about doing good in the Christian charitable organisation sense. I guessed that he was doing only himself good.

"The hug?" Tex Fraser repeated, "Well, there's something, now. I don't know as how I can explain it. And I can't show you unless I'm standing up, and you standing up, too, sort of half in front of me –"

"Now, now, Tex," I said, facetiously, "None of your homosexual business."

Blue-Coat Tex Fraser laughed.

"No," Tex Fraser said, "It's not like what you think. The hug is very easy after you been showed a few times. It ain't what you think. What I means is as I can't show you here, where we is sitting down. But I'll show you just before fall-in. You got to be standing up, and me, too."

He demonstrated the trick to me, just before we got back into line, and I could see it was very effective. So much so that a warder, witnessing the demonstration from a distance, and not knowing that it was a friendly matter, blew his whistle and wanted to have Tex Fraser charged before the Governor for "attempting to rob a fellow-convict". But there was no such charge on the book of regulations, it was discovered. For the reason that a convict has got nothing to be robbed of.

Anyway, I learnt, then, that the hug consists of another man getting hold of you from behind, when you are walking down a dark street – and preferably a bit drunk, too, although this is not altogether essential. The man who puts the hug on you sneaks up from behind. He throws his right arm around your neck, from behind, and he rests his fingers on your left shoulder, quite lightly. At the same moment he sticks a knee into the back of your left leg. Then he's got you where he wants you. If you start struggling he just rests the fingers of his right hand a little less lightly on your left shoulder, thereby shooting his forearm heavily in under your chin, making it go back higher than the stars and making you feel you're getting strangled. And all the time he's got his left hand free, enabling him to go through your pockets more or less like he wants to. That, according to the way Tex Fraser demonstrated it to me on the stone-pile, was the hug.

"So I done my dash with the sand-bag," Tex Fraser was explaining, "I made up me mind, there and then, that I wasn't going to do no more sand-bagging. That was just before – or was it just after? – I met Maggie Jones. Yes, there was a moll for you. She was *all* moll, if you knows what I mean. Nothing of the shelf or the police informant about her. And so I decides to go straight, of course. I won't go in for any game except the hug, I decides. All the crook stunts they can keep, I say."

"But why did you give up sand-bagging?" I asked, "I thought you were doing quite well hitting people over the head with a sand-bag?"

"It was because of that red-faced miner," Blue-Coat Tex Fraser pursued, "I was following him all the way down End Street. I walked after him out of the Glossop. I had a nice little sock on me, all neatly filled with sand from a mine-dump. We used to say, in the slogging game, that for miners mine-sand was the best, and that was in the days when miners was getting over two hundred pounds in their pay-cheques, end of each month. And this was the end of the month and I was follering his miner down to the bottom end of End Street. And all this time I don't get a chance to slog him. Every time I got the old sand-bag raised, a coloured person or a policeman or a liquor-seller comes past me in the dark. So I knows what it is going to be, and that it is going to finish up as a roomer. Afterwards the miner, who has had a lot to drink and is staggering plenty, comes to a long row of rooms. And all this time I don't get a chance to slog without some goat showing up. Then the miner turns in at a little gate and in at the door of a room. I toddles in after him. One time I was just going to cosh, but the top of the door-frame gets in the way. The game looks crook. What you want to pull a roomer for, when you can cosh a man in the street? And this miner goes and he lies right down on his bed, and I can see as how he is single and lives in that room by himself. I douses the glim and I goes up to the bed. The moon is shining through the window, partly, and on to the bed, just where the miner's head is. This time I got him. I hoists the old sand-bag, and I brings it down, bash, right on that miner's

99

clock. And what do you think happens? The sand-bag splits Yes, it does a bust wide open, and the soft mine-sand starts trickling out of that bust sock, and flows all over the miner's face. And he got a red face. Even in the moonlight you can see how red-faced that miner is. And the sand starts flowing over his cheek and his moustache, and he gets tickled. And there, with me bending over him, still holding on to a broken sand-bag and the sand running over his clock, tickling him, that red-faced miner bursts out laughing in his sleep.

"So I ducks out of that room quick, without waiting to collect anything, not even the sand out of the sand-bag. But I'll never forget that feeling what I got. Coshing that red-faced miner over the clock with the sand-bag, and all he does is burst out laughing. All the way down the street, as I ducked, I still hears that miner laughing.

"So I does me dash with the sand-bag. I goes in for the hug, instead. And I am still doing the hug when I meets Maggie. Jones. Maggie thinks at first as I works on the trams as a greaser. But afterwards she finds out through a john what comes up and pulls my rep to her, that I works the hotels looking for miners with pay-checks that I puts the hug on –"

It was a long story that Tex Fraser told me, the story of his love for Maggie Jones, and I am trying to find some way of condensing it. Perhaps I should explain that it was an Enoch Ardenish sort of theme.

Anyway, Maggie Jones tried to reform Tex Fraser (that was before he had got even his first blue-coat) and he had responded reasonably well, and they were madly in love with each other, and she used to work in a clothing factory down City and Suburban way, and she had a room where he came to visit her, and she said she would always love him, and that even if he found that he couldn't go straight, it wouldn't make any difference to her (although her dream was to see him become an honest man) and that whatever happened, she would always be his, if he went to prison, even. (How on earth, I wondered, could Maggie Jones have thought of so remote, so utterly unlikely a contingency?) However long he got, he would find her waiting for him, patiently and in chastity. Whenever he came out he had merely to find her: wherever she was, she would be his.

One day the johns got him.

"It was a miner what had over a hundred leaves on him. But the johns jumped on me the minute I hands him the hug. And it's seven years. And I done most of them seven years. I cracked a screw, that time I was doing my stretch, and I didn't get much remission. But I knew Maggie Jones would be waiting for me. So I goes down to City and Suburban, and they tells me Maggie is married more than five years, and she has several kids, and her husband is a blacksmith, and she stays in Jeppes. They gives me the address. I finds my way there. I know I only got to say, "It's Tex", and she'll leave her husband and kids and house: all just like that. Just on the turn. I knows Maggie. I knows she would of married that blacksmith just because she was sorry for him, and the both of them lonely. But just let her pipe little old Tex Fraser. Just once. She's my moll. My moll and no one else's moll.

"I finds the house. It's half brick and half iron. There's a little path up to the front door. And on both sides of the path is flowers. And there's two little green curtains before the windows. And in the back I hear kids' voices. And I says to myself that Maggie Jones is my moll, all the same. I just got to whistle, and she'll come running. I just got to say, "Maggie, this is Tex back," and she'll forget her husband and kids right on the turn. But as I goes up to the door I starts thinking. May-

101

be this man she married is only a blacksmith. But he's given her this nice little home. And I knows as I can't ever give Maggie anything. With me she'll be on the lam all the time. She'll have to be telling the police all sorts of tales as to where I was night before last. I can't pull her out of this, I says. And I gets to the verandah, and right up to the front door. But I don't knock. I make up my mind right away.

"And just as I am turning back the front door opens. It's Maggie. She says she heard the gate creak. She says that for months, now, each time she hears the gate creak she thinks it's me. And she come up to me with her arms out, and she says, 'I've been waiting for you for seven years. I knew you would come.' But I pushes her away, oh, very soft, and I don't say a word, but I walks out down the garden-path, and out of the little gate painted green, and I never looks back ... And to think as I never even kissed her."

I was moved by Blue-Coat Tex Fraser's story, hearing it from his own lips, there in the stone-yard, seated beside him with a pile of stones in front of us. Tex Fraser could see that I was touched by the narrative, and what made me feel somewhat suspicious of the author's sincerity was the fact that at the same time that he was keeping his hammer going up and down, grasping it in his right hand, his left hand was beginning to feel along the back of my legs: for I was sitting close to Tex Fraser.

"Yes," the blue-coat added, "And I didn't never even kiss her."

His hand kept on travelling. I got uneasy. "Edge that, Tex," I said, shifting away.

4

A subject which I found engrossed the minds of all convicts, first offenders or otherwise (indeed, next to the subject of women or dagga or good-looking young men it held first place in all discussions) was the question of a special discharge. A special discharge, in terms of practical realities, meant nothing less than that the Minister of Justice should be afflicted by a moment of aberration, and that, as a result of that mental lapse, he should automatically release some convict or other from the Swartklei Great Prison.

The possibilities of a special discharge were always extensively canvassed. The release of a man from prison through the instrument of a special discharge always excited the most exuberant kind of joy on the part of every convict. What man number one could do, man number thirty-three seventy-eight (B) could also accomplish. If one man could get out of prison, (no matter what were the means employed by the people working outside in order to obtain this result) it meant that another man could get out as well. There was a time (with Tielman Roos as Minister of Justice), when special discharges were so much the order of the day, that the Swartklei Great Prison became invested with an almost magical atmosphere. It was like in Apuleius's "The Golden Ass". Things were no longer what they seemed. You had entered an enchanted land. It was all the most marvellous make-believe. You were in and yet you weren't. Any moment you might be made an emperor. Any moment a warder might come up to you, while you were seated in a workshop, and he would instruct you to put on your jacket and to bring your hat, and to get ready to present your ticket, and you would say to him, "Is it a visitor for me, Meneer?" and he would answer in laconic tones, "No, you are for special discharge."

Naturally there were those among the more realistic of the convicts who professed to entertain a good measure of scepticism in regard to any of their number being granted a special discharge. They would say things like this, for instance, "A special discharge? Does old Bill think he'll get a special discharge? The only special discharge he'll get is through the back gate."

This was a saturnine reference to a way of leaving the Great Prison with which we had grown tolerably familiar, vicariously.

Then some other prison wit would attach a more erudite significance to the term "special discharge".

"Beauty Bell's brother has got a special discharge."

"Gawd! Can't he see a doctor about it? How long has he had it?"

Other comment in the same vein would vary from, "Well, I hope he doesn't come and discharge all over me," to "Anyway, it isn't the first time he's had a discharge up him: I dunno that it's so special, though."

But that was all just on the surface, of course. Whenever you heard that anybody had got a special discharge, you felt, "There, with a bit of luck (or influence) go I."

5

We worked very hard, in the stone yard, after those large-scale excavation and wall-building operations started. And I know that I was not the only one, but that there were many of us – we said so, to one another – who looked back with regret on the old days, when you could sit in front of a banker, and keep on chopping stones, and tell stories of the outside world, and only now and again a screw would shout, "Shut up, you ———."

When they started rearing that wall, we who were not tradesmen had to mix large quantities of mortar. I never knew what the various kinds of mortar were. I only knew there were lots of different varieties. I didn't know what they consisted of.

I could only tell by the colour of the various kinds of sand that this sort was meant for putting between the bricks, and that sort was meant for inside plaster, and that this colour stuff was used for grouting up. But I never knew what was the difference in composition – white sand, river sand, No. 3 crushed stone, cement – between one batch and another. I could only tell that one batch differed from the other by the final colour of the huge mound that we had raised in our midst, turning the lime and soil, and occasionally, stone or cement, over and over again in our shovels.

The process of mixing the mortar was always the same. A batch of sand and what you have was made into mortar as follows: one convict head would say to the other convicts, "Five sacks of cement." Then we would fetch along five sacks of cement. Or he would say, "Two coco-pans of river sand," and we would bring it along. Then the warder would say how much lime or what else. (They worked it all out in terms of formulae, and out of books of weights and measures and cubic contents and capacities, and things.) And I admired them very much, and at a suitable distance: I admired very much the stern and professional manner in which they would work out quantities together, the head screw and the convict head, a civil engineer who was doing three years for forgery. And I noticed – and so did other convicts, also – that whenever there was a dispute between these two, as to how many coco-pans, or how many shovelfuls of cement, then, in the end, the warder would always defer to the ex-civil-engineer convict, who was only doing three years. This circumstance, of course, bucked us convicts up no end. We saw, every day almost, a situation in which an ordinary convict, doing three years for forgery, was teaching a head screw how to calculate. The head screw would say, "Well I make it as we needs another six sacks of cement," and the convict-head would say, "I beg to differ, sir. I say, six-*teen* sacks, sir. You have in your addition omitted to carry over from the units into the tens, sir." And the head-screw would say, "Well, Gair, old boy," and Jimmy Gair would push his chest out, and would look side-long to see whether the rest of us convicts were taking in all the juicy details of those goings-on. And, of course, we were, and how it gave us standing, that the head screw should listen to a convict and we only in the stone-yard!

"Well I dunno, Gair," the head-screw would say again, and Jimmy Gair would look more perked than ever, because the head screw had twice called him by his name and not by his number, which was easy for the head screw to read on Jimmy Gair's shirt. It's always flattering for a convict to find himself addressed by his name, by a warder, instead of by his number. So you can imagine how Jimmy Gair, the ex-civil-engineer-convict, doing three years for forgery, must have felt. He beamed all over the place. Because it was not an ordinary discipline staff warder that was calling him by his name, but a real head screw.

And the head screw after arguing for a little bit – for half-an-hour so – during which time he was friendly in every way, never allowing the argument to get heated and contenting himself, playfully, with calling Jimmy Gair a goat and a convict that wasn't even on groceries yet, and other names like that – in the end the head screw would pucker up his forehead and say,

"Well, Gair, I know as you are the biggest simpleton we ever had in this boob, not forgetting Daft Billy Kelmer," – and those of us who remembered Daft Billy Kelmer would look at each other and smile knowingly, and those of us who didn't know about Daft Billy Kelmer would just smile – "but I don't mind saying as I think here, in this instance, in this one instance, now, mind you, I wouldn't be surprised if in spite of the dishonest weaknesses in your brain, that we all know of – I wouldn't be surprised if you really fluked this just right ... Come on, bring up sixteen sacks of cement, you lazy set of mangy dogs, you. What you stand around for idling?"

And we would bustle around and we would bring up the cement and the white sand and the lime and the river sand and the unsifted sand and all the rest of the stuff, in accordance with our instructions, until the colour of the batch, the way I worked it out, would be all right for inside plaster, and during all this time we would think, well it's not so bad being a convict, after all, when you see the way Jimmy Gair stands up to the head screw – (whose name, by the way, was Vinkel). And we would think, well, well, we may be only convicts, and all we are supposed to do is turning this mortar round and round, sweating here with these heavy shovels on the mixing-floor, but how do you like an ordinary convict like Jimmy Gair showing Head-Screw Vinkel, and in black and white, mind you, all on paper, just where this pot-bellied Vinkel gets off, anyway?

This reflection was a source of living inspiration to us. It made us convicts who had been relegated to the stone-yard, and who were looked upon as scum, on that account, suddenly feel that we weren't so unimportant a part of the prison, after all. We had a convict-head, right here in our midst, with a brain and education that was as good as that of a second-class head screw.

I remember a blue-coat coming up to me and talking to me in this strain. "What do you think of Jimmy Gair?" he asked me, proudly. And I said, yes, he was a great asset to the stone-yard. I said that we all felt, as stone-yard convicts, that we were greatly privileged to have Jimmy Gair in our span. He reflected very great honour on the stone-yard, I said.

"And another thing," the blue-coat said, "Jimmy Gair is doing only three years. What do you think of that? He's only a short-timer, only doing three years, and he's got the head screw all dippy, running around in circles. Only a short-timer, mind you. A short-*timer*. And what do you think you and I don't know, hey, what you think we couldn't do, also, hey, you and me, we that's long-timers?"

And I would agree with him, of course. And I would say that I didn't want to talk about myself at all. What claims did I have to being a long-timer, when I was doing only ten years? But that he himself was, after all, doing the blue-coat. And if a man doing three years, a lousy short three years, could have so much knowledge, like what Jimmy Gair had got knowledge, then how much more knowledge didn't we have, seeing we were long-timers, I and the blue-coat. We weren't jealous of the impression Jimmy Gair had made, of course. We were very grateful for everything that he had done to enhance the standing of the stone-yard. But it gave us a deep, inner satisfaction to realise that Jimmy Gair was only a short-timer, and that we, who were long-timers, had not spoken yet. If a man who was doing only three years knew enough to be able to make a head screw pull up his socks, what didn't we know, then, we who were doing the blue-coat, or ten years, or twenty years, or natural life?

And then when we had made a hole in the centre of the batch of mortar-mixture, and we threw bucket after bucket of water into this hole, and we moved our backsides very quick to get the mud shovelled over from one side to the other – our shovels moving a whole hill of clay over to one side as though it was porridge – then when the warders rapped out abusive comments, we were able to think, even when it felt as though our backs were breaking or that the shovels were leaden burdens that we were trying to lift with paralysed arms, we could still remember that we had a convict-head who could at any time tell the head screw to think again before he ordered six cements instead of sixteen. And this convict wasn't doing such a very long time, either.

6

I had a terrific urge for life. It was an urge that burnt me up like a lump of wood gets burnt up in a kitchen coal-stove. Life! You got no idea what a wild, fanatical zest I had for the mere thing called living. And this thing knocked hell out of me.

There was a young fellow, Donald Hughes. He worked in the mat shop. He had been in prison quite a number of times. He was an hotel-thief. The mat-shop was quite near to the stone-yard, so that we used to make use of the same open latrines, at times, Donald Hughes and I. And we would talk, in furtive whispers, about the wonder of being some day discharged from prison.

"That's where I envy you," I said to Donald Hughes, who was rather a superior type of convict, and rarely smoked dagga, "You have known what it is like to go out of prison, a free man. You have had those feelings. That is where I envy you. It must be the most wonderful feeling in the world, that experience of being told that you can go, now."

We were seated side by side in the open latrines on the edge of the bone-yard, that were shared by the convicts from quite a number of shops in the vicinity. There was a funny way of indicating to the screw that you wanted to go and relieve yourself. You held up a piece of paper in your hand, fluttering it above your head, and if the screw thought that you weren't just swinging the lead (but you were always swinging the lead, of course), then he would nod his head and you went to the latrine, the latrine-warder checking in from what shop you came and noting how long you spent sitting on the bucket. I had quite a number of interesting talks in that way, with convicts from other shops. We would sit on the buckets, talking, side by side, with the latrine warder (—house screw, we called him), timing us. And it was under these conditions that my acquaintance with Donald Hughes of the mat-shop blossomed into friendship. Now I come to think of it, the only time I ever spoke to him was when we were using the latrines. Now I think back I realise that I can only remember Donald Hughes from the way he would sit on a bucket, half forward, sort of, with his belly pulled in, straining. If I were to see him in a street, walking about, I am sure I wouldn't recognise him. I would only be able to recognise him if I saw him sitting in a lavatory.

"Yes, it is very wonderful, being discharged from boob," Donald Hughes said, "You got no idea. Being able to walk into a tobacconist's. And the girl behind the counter has got to serve you. You put down the money and you ask for whatever brand of cigarettes you want, and she has got to supply you. She can't say to you, no, you are an ex-convict; your money is no damned good. She's got to hand you what you ask for, and your change, just like you are any white man in this country. You got no idea how bucked you feel with yourself when that happens."

"I can picture to myself all sorts of things," I made answer, "There is nothing in this world that I can't sort of encompass with my imagination. But there is only one thing that I can't imagine, and that I dare not think about, even, because I feel I am not worthy of it, and that is that moment when I walk out of the front gate, and the screw at the front gate shakes hands with me, and warns me not to come back again, and I walk down the street, dressed in clothes, like what people outside wear – a jacket and trousers, and a shirt and shoes and a tie – oh, Lord, what a bright-coloured tie I want to wear on that day. But I dare not think of it. I am afraid to let my mind dwell on that possibility, even for a moment. I'm afraid of going mad, at the thought of how wonderful those moments are going to be for me, when my time is done, and I walk out of these gates, through the front, a free man."

"I been discharged several times," Donald Hughes reassured me, "And you can take it from me, it's —— marvellous, the feelings you get when you walk out there. No matter if you've done only six months. And it doesn't matter, either, how often you have been in boob. You get those same feelings every time. And when you sit in a tram, and a girl comes and sits next to you. Or you go into a bioscope café, and you sit next to a girl, and you are allowed to, and she doesn't move away, but lets you go on sitting there, right next to her, so near that you can touch her, even, if you want to . . . Gawd, the first time that happened to me, after I done two years, you got no idea how I felt. I was an ex-con. I had done two years. I had finished a couple that same morning. I had walked out of the boob, down the road, and I had took a tram into the middle of Swartklei. And that evening I went into a bioscope café. And I went and sat down next to a girl. And when the lights went on I saw she was dressed all in pink. And until to-day I couldn't tell you if she was pretty or if she wasn't. I only know that I went on sitting there, right next to her, and sometimes she moved in her seat, and her arm or her elbow would touch me, by accident, and it was heaven. You got no idea. To this girl I was a man. Not an ex-con, but a man that had every right to sit down there, in the dark, right next to her, and she not afraid I was going to rape her. It was too wonderful, you got no idea. She wouldn't go out into the street and fetch a policeman, and tell him I was an ex-con and I was sitting next to her for an hour in a bioscope café, and she dressed all in pink. And she was wearing some sort of perfume, I dunno what it's called, but it would come over me, at times, during that hour when we were sitting there, watching the film, and that perfume nearly made me go mad, it was so lovely –"

"Get back to your shops you two," the latrine warder shouted, "I been timing you. Wipe your —— and get off them buckets in two seconds or I'll report yous to the chief for loafing in the latrines."

This was a rather serious offence; so Donald Hughes and I got moving pretty quickly. But we had lots more interesting talks before he got discharged.

7

One day a warder died. It was an ordinary, natural death. He died in his house on the prison reserve, of disease, with his wife and children around him, at the last. And so the convicts had a half-holiday. Whenever a warder gets buried the convicts get a half-holiday, so as to enable the other screws to attend the funeral. But a half-holiday in the Great Prison for the convicts is a silly thing, really. Because it simply means that you don't go back into the workshops after lunch. That's all a half-holiday consists of. You stay locked up in your cage from after midday right through until the next morning. If you had to work it would have been better. You would have had some sort of a break, anyway. But staying locked up in a cage that you can just about stand up to your full height in, and that's only four or five feet wide, and that's just long enough for you to lie down in – well to my mind that was always a very poor idea of a half-holiday.

Anyway, this warder died in his house on the reserve – of pneumonia, I think it was – and the other screws all said what a shame that such a fine fellow should be cut off in his prime, and the convicts all said, well, that's one bastard less, anyhow. And so we had a half-holiday.

But there was something about this funeral of the dead screw that I couldn't quite get over, somehow. It shows how queer your mind can get after a year or two in prison, when you get used to reasoning, day after day, along the same lines, and following out the same unvarying routine from month to month and year to year. I had seen what happened to convicts that died. Whether they died natural deaths in the prison hospital, through illness; or whether they died at the end of a rope that was too short; or whether they got killed inside the prison through murder or accident: whenever a convict died the invariable procedure was to move him out through the mortuary gate, on a wheel-barrow, with two kafir convicts doing the transporting, and with a piece of sacking thrown over the dead criminal.

It was something I had got used to. That was how life had got simplified. If you went out of the prison alive, because you had done all your time, then you walked out through the front gate. But if you went out of prison as a dead man, then you travelled out through the mortuary-gate on a wheel-barrow, with your feet sticking out from underneath a piece of hessian. There were only these two ways of finally severing your connection with the Swartklei Great Prison.

And that was something I could not reconcile with the procedure that followed on the death of that warder, who had been a discipline screw in the mat shop, and whom I had seen practically every day for almost three years, and who had given me a good deal of lip, too, at intervals. I couldn't understand how they could just take him away, out of the house in which he had died, putting him in a coffin and driving him away to the cemetery in a hearse, with the mourners following in a procession.

I genuinely couldn't understand a man getting out of the prison that way. Especially that particular discipline screw in the mat shop, seeing that he had been in the prison service for close on to fifteen years.

Because he had died while in the prison service, I expected to see him come out through the mortuary gate, on a wheelbarrow and with sacking over all of him but his feet. So I never really got myself to believe that that discipline screw in the mat shop was dead, actually. That's an example of the queer sort of effect that prison can have on your mind. And while we were locked up, on that afternoon of the half-holiday we had for the screw's funeral, even then I couldn't picture what was going on outside, his corpse being removed from his house to the funeral parlour, and the coffin and the hearse and the cortège. At three o'clock that afternoon – the time of the funeral – I pictured him being wheeled out through the mortuary gate by two black convicts . . . But because I hadn't actually *seen* this happen, I never really believed that he was dead.

Chapter 6

THE GOING IN the stone-yard got rougher as the weeks passed. The excavation of the hillside and the building of the high prison wall went on side by side with the preparation of the foundations for a vast new set of workshops, designed on modern lines. The screws, just as much as the convicts, were getting into a state of nerves at all this unwonted activity. Perhaps even the master-tradesman had begun developing a nostalgia for the old days, when over the stone-yard there had hung an air of comparative repose. The work was not going according to plan, somehow. All sorts of mistakes were constantly being made. These mistakes, when detected, had to be hurriedly rectified before the master-tradesman jerried to them. The master-tradesman, in turn, seemed to be getting chivvied by the Commissioner of Public Works and the architect, and, for all we knew, by the Prime Minister. For it is a singular fact, this, that to every convict inside the place, the Swartklei Great Prison is the hub of the nation's life. A convict genuinely believes that no new piece of legislation, whether it is a new Flag Bill or whether it deals with foreign trade, is ever brought before Parliament before its probable effect on the Swartklei Great Prison has been carefully taken into account.

Thus you can say to almost any convict, "Why doesn't the Government introduce the decimal system?" and he will answer, without knowing anything about it, "Well, of course, the boob won't stand for it." Or you can ask any man in prison, "What is the railway administration doubling the line to Odendaalsrus for?" and he'll inform you, straight on the turn,

"Well, isn't that how the boys in the Great want it?"

But the master-tradesman, every time he got bullied over the job, passed it on to the trades-warders, and they in turn chewed the ears off the discipline screws, who got busy on the convicts. The discipline screws made us sweat all right. And the most ridiculous things seemed to be happening, all the time. One morning they lost a couple of tons of dressed stone. They looked for that dressed stone all over the place. The stones had been loaded and taken, somewhere, but nobody knew where, or in what. When the stones were discovered, eventually it was found that a trades-warder had been sitting on them most of the morning, trying to puzzle out, on a plan that he had spread in front of him, in what part of the excavations the stones could have been off-loaded.

And the remarks the trades-warders made all sounded sensible, but when you got to analysing the things they said you found they were talking rather a lot of tripe.

"Those —— stones couldn't have been stolen," a screw would say, "I mean there's four men with guns on the parapet, and if a lot of stones went out from here, somebody would have *seen* them go out."

And another screw would say, "It's since they done away with the silence system, that everything goes wrong in the boob. Give me the old days when the only word you heard out of a convict was 'Yes, sir'. If they still had the silence system them stones wouldn't a got lorst."

And the convicts would say, amongst each other, facetiously, "I suppose the stones been bottled (meaning smuggled) through into the section. The bottling is getting worse every day." Or another one would say, "This is where they want the police. Ring up headquarters and ask for two johns and a trap-boy and a couple of bleeding blood-hounds. Let the johns go sniffing around the boob for them dressed rocks." And another convict said, "I bet if the blood-hounds comes, I bet they follows a trail into old Head-Screw Vinkel's back-yard." And the convicts who heard that remark broke into guffaws, it being suspected that Head-Warder Vinkel on occasion was not above taking prison tools and materials home for his own use. "Funny if the johns comes to the boob, after them stones," a blue-coat muttered significantly, "And they starts searching the screws' houses on the reserve. They'll find a lot more than dressed stones." There followed a chorus of voices enumerating articles allegedly stolen out of the prison by the warders:

"They'll find refrigerators."

"And pots of paint."

"And saws and hammers and screw-drivers and braces and bits and –"

"And turning lathes."

"And lavatory-seat tops."

"And beds and tables and chairs and cups and knives and spoons."

"And big parcels of dagga."

"And silk dressing-gowns. And silver cruet-stands. And embroidered table-cloths."

If the convicts did not have to talk to each other out of the sides of their mouths, all this would have created bedlam. As it was, all that broke the silence was a lot of voices saying things at the same time, and these voices coming out sideways from between half-closed lips: it made a funny picture, really. And it didn't seem to occur to the convicts until a good while afterwards, that they were accusing the warders of having stolen things that never had been (and never would be, alas) found in any kind of prison at all. By the way they spoke, handing out a list of all the things they had seen stolen out of the Swartklei

Great Prison by warders at various times, it sounded as though the prison was some Eastern potentate's palace that had been looted by a barbarian hill-tribe.

I can only say that during all the time I was in the Swartklei Great Prison, I never once saw a warder steal anything. I only once saw a warder as much as pick up a piece of soap. And then he caught my eye, and he grinned sort of foolishly, and he put the piece of soap back again, exactly in the place where he had found it, and he wiped his hand on the side of his trousers, because it had been a piece of wet soap.

I believe that the tradition among convicts that the warders steal just about everything within sight is actually based on some sort of vicarious day-dreaming – something to do with wish-fulfilment, and frustrations and the like. From my own observation I cannot say that I ever found much evidence to corroborate the widely-held belief (among convicts), that most of the honest people are inside and most of the dishonest people are outside, and that a convict, by his nature, is more honest (and conspicuously so) than a prison-warder.

Anyway, lots of mistakes kept on being made. The foundations had been laid in the wrong place. This meant new sets of trenches having to be dug and to be filled with concrete. It wasn't so much the wasted labour that the master-tradesman objected to, when the architect showed him where he had gone wrong (for it had been his job in the first place to mark out where the foundations had to go) but what made him go red in the face was the thought of all those sacks of cement and tons of crushed stone. And so the master-tradesman passed on the vexation he felt on account of his own mistake. He passed his indignation on to the senior trades head-warder, who in turn let old Vinkel have a mouthful. And so down the line. By the time the master-tradesman's dissatisfaction struck us convicts labouring on the stone-pile, it was something pretty terriffic. The discipline screws didn't let up one moment in sassing us around. Almost every five minutes you heard, "Where's your ticket?" and a screw would take a convict's ticket from him, and have him marched to the Governor's office, charged with idling, and it meant three days' solitary confinement on spare diet every time. In their anxiety to show the master-tradesman how far they had identified themselves with his feelings, some of the discipline warders would go out of their way to boot some refractory convict soundly in the rear, whenever they thought the master-tradesman was looking. In their zeal to impress the master-tradesman, these discipline screws went somewhat outside the strict fetter of the Prison Regulations, which laid it down that a convict could prefer a charge against a warder if the warder shot him (the convict) around with his boot.

But, of course, no convict would ever be so foolish as to "prefer a charge" against a warder. That phrase sounds exquisite to me, somehow. Imagine a convict going up to a prison Governor (whom he can't even interview unless he has obtained permission from the hall head-warder, and from the reception-office chief-warder and I don't know from whom else) and then the convict says to the Governor, "Please, sir, I wish to prefer a charge against Mr. Prison-Officer Pistorius." Personally, I can't conceive of a thing like that happening. But if a convict did get so far it would be more than a warder's boot up his backside that would send him back across the hall. And quite right, too. If I was a prison Governor, I wouldn't hold any brief, either, for a man who came up to me and squealed. A man who narks on a warder can just as easy, next time, come his guts on a fellow-con.

There's got to be a certain rough-and-ready discipline in a

prison and it isn't as though you get booted by every screw in the boob every day. And it isn't as though this booting practice gets contagious or sets a bad example to others. For instance I've seen lots of clergymen coming into the boob to conduct services on Sundays: and I've never seen one of these clergymen (through imitating the bad example of the warders) ever go up to a convict and boot him up the backside or in the ribs. Rather would the kindly prison-chaplain hand the benighted convict an uplifting tract. Instead of lifting him one.

Anyway, I've never yet come across an instance of a convict being so misguided as to go and "prefer a charge" against a screw for getting playful in the stone-yard. Nor, as a convict, would I have liked to volunteer to give evidence for the convict laying the charge. I would rather have said that a bit of lime-dust flew into my eye, just then, and that I hadn't seen anything. I certainly wouldn't have wanted to give evidence against a warder. I didn't want to be a marked man among the screws in any other sense than that I was a longtimer.

The rough-neck sort of prison-warder who was a bit free with his baton or his boot was always much more popular than the other sort, who would come up to you from behind, quietly, and in polite tones ask you for your ticket, please. None of the convicts could stand that kind of warder, whose lips would be thin and in a straight line, and who would be a real sadist. An illiterate old screw like Vinkel or "Spoons" would as likely as not listen when you told him a pathetic story. He would quite possibly relent if you said, "Please, meneer, will you give me back my ticket? If I get charged I lose my privileges for the month, and so my mother won't be able to visit me next Tuesday. And she's coming all the way from Cape Town, meneer."

As likely as not a screw like "Spoons" would give you back your ticket on a tale like that. A tight-lipped, sadistic screw with quiet ways, never.

2

It was a winter morning, but the sweat was already beginning to run off our bodies, the way the screws kept us on the move. I was with a span that was shovelling over a batch of mortar on the mixing-floor.

"That stuff is still raw," I heard a voice at my ear, "Don't go to sleep on the bleeding job." The words came out of a mouth opened sideways. So I knew it wasn't a screw talking to me. I went on shovelling. After a while I answered, "Don't you give me no blasted orders. You're just a convict like me. You're not promoted to a screw."

I didn't know yet who was ordering me around. I only knew it wasn't a warder. By way of reply, the convict who had the cheek to criticise my work lifted his shovel and brought the bowl flat down on the handle of my shovel, as though by accident. My shovel went spinning into the batch of mortar. There was laughter from the convicts around me. I went and retrieved my shovel, wiping the mud off the handle on the lower part of my jersey. And then I saw that the convict who was getting fresh with me was none other than Slangvel. I got a bit scared, then. Slangvel was in general an easy-going sort of person, secure in his physical strength, and not easily moved. But his impudence in picking on me like that, just for nothing, infuriated me. He must be full of dagga. I felt terrible. If another convict could start giving me orders, God knew where it would end up. I would be working in a place where everybody would be my boss, from the Governor down to anybody doing six months.

"You do your work proper or I'll bust you," Slangvel announced when I had got back into line. He was still speaking sideways.

Slangvel was bouncing me. I was scared to bounce him back. "Turn it up, Slangvel," I said, "We're all doing time, man. I don't want any trouble, even if you do."

"You do your time proper, then," Slangvel answered, "Don't work like a blooming kafir and leave all them raw pieces of lime –"

He was blue with dagga, of course. And in his dagga-riddled brain there was no doubt some sort of hallucination, at that moment, that he was in prison to keep an eye on the way I worked. It was getting bad, and I was scared. But I had to stick to my guns.

"And if I don't take orders from you," I asked, "then what?"

Before I had finished speaking the shovel again flew out of my hands, and there was more laughter from the other convicts. Slangvel, man of muscle, did not need words for conveying his ideas.

Anyway, this little interlude came to a somewhat abrupt end, at the back of the tool-shed, a little later, when the mortar was mixed and we were transporting it in wheel-barrows.

Slangvel and I were facing each other, with half-a-dozen convicts from our span standing around us, and a couple of convicts standing some distance away to keep longstall on the warders.

Slangvel made a rush at me. I got out of the way of his rush, somehow, and he charged on for a few yards, almost colliding with a wheel-barrow. His neck bulged. His eyes were shot with red veins, from excessive dagga-smoking. I had punched at him, as he went careering past me, and I had missed. I felt that even if I had landed him a crack it would have had just about no effect on him. I knew that if Slangvel landed me a solid crack, on the jaw with one of his flying fists, or in the groin with a boot, it would just about be lights-out for me. I wasn't worried about that. I was only scared of what Slangvel would do to me with his boots once he got me down. He was dagga-mad. He was like an infuriated bull. You could see it in his eyes. I had to do something. And quick. I was in a dangerous situation. I felt that if Slangvel got me down he would proceed to kill me. With those boots. He wasn't a bad fellow at heart. But he had lost all control of himself. In his dagga-stupor he didn't know what he was doing. And those stone-yard convicts standing around would not have enough sense of responsibility to pull him off me, once I was down. So I started playing for time.

"Just a minute," I said, "I want to take off my jersey."

"Yah! He's yellow," a young convict, an ex-reformatory boy, exclaimed, "Donner him, Slangvel."

Nevertheless, Slangvel, out of a mistaken sense of chivalry, or because he just didn't quite know what was going on, in any case, paused. I peeled off my brown prison-jersey. Slangvel intimated that he was going to take off his jersey also. I don't suppose he really wanted to discard his jersey. I think it was merely some sort of moron-imitativeness. Perhaps he thought it was a more official sort of thing to do, taking off his jersey before beating up a man.

He tugged at the lower part of his jersey, bringing it up level with his tremendous chest. He puffed and snorted. The bottom of his jersey came up level with his chin. I saw the scar from where he had fallen on his chin, the day they had picked him up in front of the tap and had carried him into hospital. The scar on his chin was still livid. And it was the sight of this scar on Slangvel's chin that gave me an idea. It was very quick. It all took place, I should imagine, in a fraction of a second. Or it might have taken a little longer, I don't know ... But when Slangvel had pulled up his jersey above the level of his eyes, and was busy trying to jerk it off his head and shoulders, I had already got going. I picked up a five-pound stone hammer and made for Slangvel. His arms were up in the air and his head was wrapped in the folds of his jersey. So he never knew what struck him. I hit out (but not too hard) at that place inside the jersey where I imagined Slangvel's chin to be. Slangvel went down like a log. He lay on the ground, between two wheel-barrows, stretched out at full length, with the jersey still half-way round his head.

At that moment a warder, sensing that something unusual was happening, came up.

"What the hell's this?" the screw asked.

"He done fell down," the ex-reformatory boy, who a few minutes before had gee-d Slangvel on to me, explained to the screw, "He was taking off his jersey and he tripped over his big feet, meneer."

Nobody in the span narked on me. I should have known they wouldn't.

"I suppose some of you mongrels hit him," the screw said, but he didn't try to push the matter.

"Slangvel bonked his head on the wheel-barrow when he fell over his feet," another convict volunteered.

"You mustn't call a convict by his name," the warder announced pontifically, "Don't you knows your regulations? You must calls him by his number."

"But his number is inside his jersey, meneer," the convict replied, "And the other number is sewed on the back of his pants. And he's lying on his bum, meneer."

"Throw some water on him and get on with the work," the screw answered.

That ended the little incident. Slangvel revived shortly afterwards, and by fall-in time he was as right as rain. And he was docile. He worked alongside me without any display of rancour; he really seemed to bear me no ill-will. And I was no longer afraid of him. I felt that if he started with me again, I'd settle him with some more treachery.

My hitting Slangvel with the stone-hammer, in that way, when he couldn't see a thing and his arms were tangled up, aroused various reactions on the part of the convicts of the stone-yard span. One man came and gave me a doppie tobacco, afterwards. He had always wanted that big bully Slangvel lathered up, he informed me, but he also requested me not to inform Slangvel that he had said so. The ex-reformatory boy said that even in the reformatory he had never seen anything as low as hitting a man when he's got his jersey half over his head. And then hitting him with a hammer, on top of it. But then what did you expect from a first-offender, anyway?

Still, it cleared the air for me a lot, in the stone-yard, this little incident. I found that here and there, among the convict heads, my views were accorded a measure of respect which they had not enjoyed so far. What had started as an ugly-looking sort of affair ended quite harmlessly.

But there were many nights, after that, when I was lying alone in my cell in the section, and I remembered my attack on Slangvel in the stone-yard, that I was overcome with terror at the thought of what might have happened. I might have hit him too hard with the hammer and he might have died. "And the deceased, so lingering, died." All that legal terminology. And this time they wouldn't have reprieved me. I might have hit him just a little too hard with that hammer. He might have moved and I would have got him on the temple, and he would have dropped down dead. I was serving time for murder.

How would I go on another murder charge? I would think of Slangvel lying down there between the two wheel-barrows, and me still with that hammer in my hand, and the most cold and horrible nightmare fears would sweep over me.

3

After a couple of years the job of building the wall and the workshops was ended, and we in the stone-yard returned to our old routine of sitting down in long rows, chopping stones into small bits. But, like my sojourn in the printers' shop, the experience I acquired of the building-trade also stood me in good stead in later years. The knack of tipping a loaded wheel-barrow is always a useful accomplishment in life.

It took us a couple of years to build the wall and the workshops. A couple of years is all right, if you say it fast. But in prison it seems a long time. Even a short stretch seems to take a long time to do.

And talking about time, the doing it and the length of it, reminds me of what once happened in the printers' shop. The head-warder had discovered a whole lot of loose type under the floor-boards. How the type got there was in this way: through the years, whenever a convict had a job of dissing to do that bored him, he would just take a column of type and drop it through a hole in the floor, thereby saving himself the job of distributing all that stuff, letter by letter, into the various boxes. By the time the head-warder discovered that hole in the floor there was quite a mound of type lying there. The convicts all professed great interest and astonishment, averring their disapproval of the kind of person, lower than a rattlesnake's anus, who could chuck a lot of type under the floor-boards in order to save himself a bit of extra work. That sort of thing never happened in their time, they declared. It must have happened in the old days, when those Australians were in the prison, and the convicts did not have the same sense of responsibility and honour and rectitude that animated them to-day.

Anyway, the head-warder had the floor-boards torn up, and all the type was brought out from underneath, and it was all dumped into a huge box. To a convict named Botha was delegated the task of sorting all that vast chaos of type, letter by letter, into the various partitions in the type-cases. A corner in the printers' shop was specially fitted out for him. In the midst of many rows of cases, with the box full of assorted type of every variety of size and face before him, Botha would sit on a little stool, patiently picking out and distributing letters that varied from about 36-point Gillsans Bold to 6-point italic and 10-point Doric.

"How long do you reckon the job will take you?" I asked of Botha, one day.

"About seven years," he replied.

His answer frightened me a little. I thought of a man outside. What doesn't happen to a man outside prison in the course of seven years? The good years and the bad years. The adventures that come his way. The triumphs and the heart-breaks that are bound up with seven years of living. The processions of the seasons, spring succeeding winter and autumn following summer, seven times. A man could meet a girl and fall in love and get married and have quite a number of children, all in seven years. And he could get a job and get fired, and travel all over the world, and starve and succeed, and lust and weep and hate and take vengeance. All these things in all these years.

And during this time Botha the convict would be sorting the type out of the box. Only after seven years would his fingers close around the last pica space. And nothing would be happening to Botha during these years. Just nothing at all.

Another rather interesting thing happened in the printers' shop near the end of my stay there, just shortly before I was kicked out into the stone-yard. A warder named Marman, who was stationed at the local gaol, came into the printers' shop to relieve the printers' head trades-warder when he went on a month's leave. Now, the warder Marman had literary leanings. He had written a novel about prison-life. He called the novel "Die Liefdesgeskiedenis van Bloubaadjie Theron." The hero was a blue-coat. And Discipline-Warder Marman made a very noble figure out of him. He had been innocently convicted, quite a number of times, this blue-coat hero of Marman's romance, and he had never squealed, always taking the blame for what his friends or relatives did. But there was a girl who waited for this blue-coat through the years . . .

Anyway, it was a very moving story that this warder Marman wrote. It was full of slush and sentiment and melodrama and bad grammar. And he got us to print that book for him. He gave us a tin of tobacco apiece, and we worked like fury to be able to set and run off that little book, "Die Liefdesgeskiedenis van Bloubaadjie Theron," before the trades head-warder came back from his leave. Four comps did the setting. All by hand. I read the proofs. The machine-men made up and ran off each section as it was set. The cleaner washed the ink off the formes with soft-soap each time a run was completed. And Discipline-Warder Marman kept watch at the door for the chief warder or the Governor, and he would say "All correct, sir," when one of these superior officials happened along, and so nobody was the wiser. It was, I suppose, one of the biggest under-the-lap jobs ever undertaken in the prison.

About two days before the head trades-warder was due to

return from leave the job was finished. The book looked quite imposing, although the sections weren't bound, but only stitched together with wire, and with paper covers. Marman took delivery, smuggling the books out under his rain-coat, a few parcels at a time. And then we remembered something. Funny we hadn't thought of it before. There were many pages of this book still standing in type. The letters hadn't been distributed into the cases. It had been all right with the Governor and the chief warder, and the other warders of the discipline staff, who wouldn't know what was going on in the printers' shop in any case. But the moment the head trades-warder came back he would see all those pages set up in type and we would be exposed. The whole shop would be guilty. We worked like in a frenzy, dumping all that type back, letter by letter, into the various cases. But we still couldn't manage. We started chucking the letters in just anyhow, pie-ing the cases. But it was still no good. The head-warder would come back and find out what we had been up to.

Of course, there was no other solution, in the end. The floor-boards which had been carefully nailed down after the type accumulated over the years had been retrieved and given to Botha to sort, were now prised up, once more. And the remaining chapters of Discipline Head-Warder Marman's novel, in the form of column after column of loose type set by hand, were shot through the hole in the floor.

By the time the head trades-warder returned the floor-boards were nailed down again, very neatly.

4

There is another little story I would like to relate about time and the doing of it.

Donnie Graham was a young blue-coat. He was only about twenty-seven or twenty-eight. He had started on his career of crime early and had been declared an habitual criminal when his cheeks were still rosy.

One day the Governor sent for all the blue-coats. They formed up in a body in the hall, and he addressed them.

"I have just received a circular from the Department of Justice," the Governor said, "And it affects you convicts serving the indeterminate sentence. As you know, until now it has been the practice for the Board to recommend the discharge of an habitual criminal after he has served six years. No doubt, all of you are serving your sentences under the impression that you will be released after you have completed five or six years. Many of you, no doubt, also, who have completed five years, are expecting to be recommended for discharge in the course of this year. Well, I have to inform you that the regulations have been changed, and that from now on the Board of Prison Visitors will not recommend any one of you men for discharge until he has served nine or ten years. That's all. I trust what I have communicated to you is clear to every one of you. It means that from to-day onwards you will have to remain in prison four or five years longer than was previously the rule. You may go now. Are there any questions?"

Donnie Graham piped up.

"Please sir," he asked, "Can we have pepper in our beans on Fridays?"

Chapter 7

THERE WAS A TIME in the prison when the food was very bad. First it was the bread. Then the mealie-pap got bad. Afterwards you couldn't eat the carrot-soup either. The convicts expressed their disapproval in various ways. A few minor assaults were committed on some of the convicts working in the kitchen, when they brought the food into the hall on little trolleys. It didn't seem a particularly sensible sort of thing to do, assaulting the kitchen-hands. The trouble seemed to have originated much higher up. Hitting a trolley-pushing convict from the kitchen over the head with a lump of iron – specially smuggled in from the workshops for that purpose – did not achieve very much in the way of improving the quality of the fare supplied three times a day to six hundred convicts. What was more, when these trifling assaults on the kitchen-hands grew in number, the chief warder made other arrangements about transporting the meals from the kitchen into the sections: he gave instructions that half-a-dozen members from the refuse-gang had to perform that office. It is a tribute to the good sense of the convicts that I am able to record the fact that only on two occasions were refuse-span convicts offered physical violence when pushing the food-trolleys into the hall.

But on each occasion you could smell, a long distance off, how bad the food was that was coming through from the kitchen.

And there was just about nothing that we could do about it. Every lunch-time at least two dozen convicts would line up in the hall and, as an empty gesture, proclaim to the head-warder that a dog couldn't eat porridge like that. Or that the beans weren't fit for pigs. Or that an orang-outang couldn't drink that soup.

But we couldn't get much satisfaction that way. Because the fault lay with people higher up than the kitchen. Maybe higher than the stores department, even. To try and remedy the matter by means of a daily gentlemanly protest – a couple of dozen convicts gathering in the hall and showing the head-warder the contents of their dixies – was just about as futile a procedure as taking an impatient kick at one of the trolley-wheels.

A convict would say to the head-warder, "This isn't fit for a pig. Just taste it, sir."

Or another convict – equally unconscious of any innuendo – would say, "Just have a mouthful of this, sir. And tell us if you think a gorilla could swallow it."

Every time, of course, the head-warder would decline the proffered delicacy, on the pretext either that he had lunched, or that his wife was keeping lunch waiting for him, and if he ate now he wouldn't have any appetite for his food when he got home. Sometimes he simply said, straight out, that he wasn't hungry.

The only way to get better food was to demonstrate on a scale big enough to cause repercussions. Because the only satisfaction we got out of the head-warder was that he spoke severely to a number of the refuse-span convicts pushing the food-trolleys along.

"Aren't you ashamed to bring in muck like this?" he would ask these convicts, who looked pretty sheepish, in any case, having to do this extra (and slightly risky) chore.

If the warder was in a bad mood, he would wax sarcastic.

"Of course, you convicts are used to only the best when you are outside," he would say, "Of course, you are used to having skoff in only the best hotels, where you tips the waiter ten bob and he polishes your top-hats on his sleeve. And through a miscarriage of the law you're all here behind bars and missing your champagne and caviare and Havanas. Perhaps I'll get my wife to cook some invalid soup for you big, strapping hoboes. And I'll smuggle the soup inside in a wash-tub hid under my tunic."

And we'd think, yes, we'd like to know what he hasn't in his time already smuggled into – and out of – the prison.

But we didn't say what we thought, of course, and the head-warder wouldn't say much more, either, except that at the end of his little speech he would remark, "Now, beat it, you bums."

But when he was in a really bad humour, the head-warder would get threatening, and he would say, "Now, you get to hell out of it, the whole two dozen of you. Or I'll charge you before the Governor for making frivolous complaints."

And there were those among the convicts who said that he would charge them, also. But he would have to write out a charge-sheet, and he would have to fill in the nature of the charge he was bringing. And the head-warder didn't know how to spell "frivolous", the convicts said. But this was another thing that they didn't say to his face, either. Looking at that head-warder, I would wonder, idly, sometimes, as to how exactly he *would* spell the word "frivolous." In a highly frivolous way, no doubt.

The upshot of it was that there were a few demonstrations. I would hardly say that these demonstrations were well-organised. The convicts did a number of spontaneously imitative things. One morning, for instance, all the portions of bread were flung into the hall. First one convict, standing on an upstairs landing overlooking the hall, pushed his bread through the bars and flung it down on to the floor below. Then another convict followed his example. In a few moments dozens of convicts were doing the same thing, pieces of soggy bread flying about the hall and landing on the head-warder's desk and messing up the floor, and landing near the head-warder, too, some of the bits. There was a terrific crush on the balconies at the end of the sections overlooking the hall, every convict dutifully bringing along his portion of bread and thrusting it through between the bars and sending it flying down into the hall. But it wasn't so much a sense of loyalty, perhaps, that animated the convicts in their participation in this gesture of convict solidarity over the food question. It was just that it was fun to be able to commit an outrage like this, when there was something sort of sacrosanct about the hall, and it was jolly to be able to be defiant like that, just for once, putting your hand through between the bars and chucking your piece of bread down into the hall – with the prospect of even getting the head-warder on the head with it.

It was a nice feeling. "Yah –!" Like that. Cocking a snook at the whole prison. Tearing a sheet off the copy of the Prison Regulations and rolling a dagga smoke in it. It gave you a wonderful sense of pure and heroic freedom, watching your own piece of bread land in the hall, down below. But now I come to think of it, it seems that it wasn't such an unreasonable thing to do with that bread. You certainly couldn't eat it.

And the head-warder in the hall was in a very good mood, that day. He didn't turn a hair.

"Waste not, want not, boys," was all he said, by way of admonition.

Nevertheless, it was a pretty sizeable demonstration. On the way out from the sections and in the workshops the convict naturally talked of nothing else.

"It was Alec the Ponce wot chucked in the first piece of bread," one convict said.

"It wasn't. It was Blue-coat Verdamp. I was standing as far off him as I am from you. And I chucked my bread in next, right after him. It was –"

"The first man that dumped his bread was a first offender. It come right down from the first offenders' section," somebody else said.

"Then it must have flew right back again," somebody interrupted him, "It couldn't come from the first offenders. The first offenders is all a lot of yellow rats, afraid to do a thing in case they loses their remission."

There were quite a number of fights in the stone-yard, that morning. It was a thorny issue. Who was to get the credit for having thought out and taken the lead in that startlingly original demonstration? It was an historical event. You ought to have seen how the hall looked. Nowhere to walk at all. Just bread all over the place. One of the convicts even swore that he saw a few bread-crumbs sticking behind the head-warder's ear, when he came close up to him. But somebody else said those crumbs were probably there from when the head-warder had breakfast, and that he had forgotten to wipe his face. This was typical of the sort of opinions that prevailed among the prisoners about the head-warder.

But the question as to which was the convict that should get the honour for having taken the initiative in chucking his piece of bread into the hall was hedged around with all sorts of difficulties. Eventually, all the other claimants having been eliminated, it was agreed that it was either Alec the Ponce or Blue-coat Verdamp that had taken the lead. And by lunch-time it was pretty generally conceded that right was right, and that whatever views you held about Alec the Ponce, it was nevertheless a fact that he had chucked his bread into the hall at least two seconds before Blue-coat Verdamp had done so.

But there were supporters of Blue-coat Verdamp who maintained, in spite of all arguments and threats, that Blue-coat Verdamp had in actual fact got in first. When he saw the way public opinion was going, Blue-coat Verdamp got sore. He couldn't understand what was wrong with the boys, he declared. He had been in prison, on and off, from the very early days. In twenty years he had spent only two Christmases outside, he said. And the boys in the game were not what they used to be.

"Alec the Ponce is only doing four and a half years, ain't he?" the Blue-coat demanded truculently, "And I am doing twice as long as him, ain't I? And what's the blasted idea giving a short-timer, what's doing only four and half years, credit over a long-timer like me? I got a good mind to go back into that hall and bring back my piece of bread."

Blue-coat Verdamp paused for a moment, then added savagely, "And eat it."

But his friends advised him not to do anything foolish. It would, of course, make Alec the Ponce and his supporters look very silly if Blue-coat Verdamp went and took back his bread and ate it.

"But you'll get very sick, man, from that bread," somebody said, "Nobody can eat that bread and not go to hospital. Not even a head-warder can eat that bread."

"And how amongst all that bread will you find your own piece?" another man asked, "For all you know, you might even pick up Alec the Ponce's piece of bread, and eat it. And how will you feel then?"

It had been quite a good demonstration, throwing the bread into the hall like that. It was a pity that what had been an historic act should have left this aftermath of bitter dissension.

Now, there are a number of rather queer things about mob psychology. And I learnt one or two somewhat singular things, during the course of the food-trouble, that McDougal seems to have left out of his text-book on psychology. For instance, after the first spontaneous expression of dissatisfaction in the form of the whole prison, including the first offenders' section, flinging its bread into the hall, nobody after that felt any kind of *mass* urge to repeat that particular kind of performance. The mass mind felt, instinctively, that future protests had to take some other form. But there were individuals, inside of this crowd of six hundred convicts, who hadn't the psychological sense to grasp this artistic truth. That was where men with the gift of leadership, like Blue-coat Verdamp and Alec the Ponce, knew their potatoes. But there were other convicts who hadn't this subtle, intuitive feeling about mob urges. One of these less highly-gifted persons was a first-offender named Winslow who had been a book-keeper in civilian life and who was now serving a sentence of three years for fraud.

It was Winslow's weakness that he was trying, in and out of season, to set up as a prison-head. He would always be first with a new rumour. When there was talk, on the occasion of some event or other of national importance, about the remission of sentence that every convict would be sure to get, then Winslow would always be the first to impart, with a very knowing sort of air, exact information as to the form that the Governor-General's clemency was going to take. And events nearly always proved him wrong. Never mind anything else, almost every time when we thought we were going to have our sentences mitigated, it turned out that we got nothing off at all. The authorities never even thought of the prison. And so with everything else. When a new convict arrived, Winslow would always take him in tow, and teach him the ropes, so as to be able to pose to this new convict that he, Winslow, was a very big and important "head", who had decided to instruct a raw new-comer in the majestic lore of a great prison, merely because he was sorry for him. But after a week or two this greenhorn first-timer would learn enough of the ropes himself to cut out Winslow, who would then again be left friendless for a while, walking up and down the exercise yard on his own.

And when there was a concert, some party of amateur singers and guitar-players from head-office entertaining the convicts for an evening, then it would always be Winslow that tried to jump up first to make the customary little speech, thanking the visitors for having come round. Naturally, this effrontery on the part of a first offender annoyed those of the old hands who had come to regard this office, of making a little speech of thanks to the concert-parties, as one of the privileges appertaining to certain select spirits who had served at least seven or eight sentences and had grown grey, so to speak, in the service of the prison. The result was that after he had been struck down one night, just after he had jumped to his feet and had got as far as "Mr. Governor and —", Winslow didn't try to make any more speeches in the hall. He was struck down with a lavatory seat specially torn from its hinges, earlier that afternoon, by some of the blue-coats in the penal section.

Incidentally, I have often wondered, since then, what the concert-party thought of that little incident. There was a banjo-player, and a man who sang deep bass songs, and an amateur magician who juggled with cards (he had a nerve, all right:

there were a number of card-sharpers among those six hundred convicts who could have shown *him* a trick or two, and not just platform tricks, but grim, real-life stuff) and half-a-dozen gentlemen who did not perform, but only sat back on the stage with their arms folded, very conscious of the fact that they were Distinguished Visitors, and that they would never land behind prison bars, of course, and a man who blew on a trumpet, and some other men who sang, but not in such deep bass tones as the first one, and a man who told funny stories. They were stories that had been told often in the prison, and for that reason they were popular stories. The convicts knew exactly when the funny part was coming, and what the point of it was, and where to laugh, which they did, each time, uproariously. No humorous stories were as popular as the well-tried chestnuts. There was one story about a coloured girl called "Wi'lets" that brought the house down, regularly, year after year. And sometimes, when the humorist omitted to tell it, because he was already sick of it, no doubt, there would be a chorus of "Wi'lets" from hundreds of convict throats (and from the throats of quite a number of warders, too), so that this amateur public entertainer from the head-office would be constrained to relate this same little anecdote about "Wi'lets", in the same words and the same intonation that he had employed year after year for upward of a decade. And next morning, on their way out to the workshops, convicts would greet each other with this catch-word, old crony calling to crony, "Wi'lets", even while they were still marching in line, and warders who were new recruits would stare in amazement, but the old hands among the warders would smile indulgently.

The bass singer rendered the same solos, too, year after year. He was, as an entertainer, second in popularity only to the raconteur. The bass vocalist sang one thing that was a noble blending of the martial with the sentimental. It was a song about an old chateau, or an old chapeau, or an old shako: nobody ever caught that word properly. And it had a powerful refrain about "Ten, twenty, thirty – *forty* – years ago." It was a lovely song. And justly popular. The convicts thought that the "ten, twenty, thirty, *forty* years ago" had reference to the date when they were last outside, and they regarded the bass singer's regular inclusion of this item in his repertoire as a graceful gesture to the long-timers.

But to return to the last occasion on which Winslow jumped up and tried to thank the concert-party. I often wondered what those gentlemen from the Department of Justice head office in the Union Buildings thought, then, when the leader of the concert-party announced that there were no further items on the programme, and one of the convicts jumped up and began a little speech with the words "Mr. Governor and –" and then suddenly a lavatory-seat swung in a wide arc made contact with the top of his head, and he subsided without another word and had to be carried feet first back into the section, while a blue-coat, almost as though by arrangement, got up and made a sonorous, old-time sort of a speech, filled with battered clichés and good feeling and bad grammar, and expressing disappointment at the fact that the authorities had not seen fit to celebrate the successful combating of the locust plague in the Kalahari, last year, by granting some remission of sentence to the long-timers.

I suppose those gentlemen from head-office, when they heard that speech and saw that lavatory-seat, and all – I suppose they just thought to themselves, "Ah, well."

No action was taken by the prison authorities against the convicts who had laid Winslow out at the concert. The warders weren't keen on a man like Winslow getting up and talking when officials from the Department of Justice were present. Not too well-educated themselves, they resented the idea that a man with some smatterings of learning should profess to represent the convicts. That wouldn't do. Where would the warders be if the idea got about in the Department of Justice that the men doing time in the prison were suave and polished and scholarly, and that the warders were a set of illiterate thugs? The warders were most happy when an after-the-concert speech was made by some stupid-looking blue-coat who drooled away for about five minutes in an incoherent form of prison slang, making homely references to his work in the mat-shop and to dietary matters.

Anyway, to return to the food disturbances ... Winslow was out of touch with public opinion in the prison. He had but little intuition about the way people thought and felt en masse. So the next morning after the incident of the bread-throwing he made rather a fool of himself. Because the credit for having flung the first piece of bread into the hall was being shared between Alec the Ponce and Blue-coat Verdamp, these two men being thereby elevated to a position of high consequence in the life of the prison, Winslow felt that here was his chance to establish himself as leader of the first offenders' section. To-day he would be the first to fling his bread into the hall. The rest of the prison would pattern after him. He would be in the limelight.

Consequently, the moment his cell-door was unlocked, Winslow dashed out with his piece of bread and made for the landing. He got there before anybody else. He couldn't sense that there was no mass feeling in favour of repeating the demonstration of the day before. And he threw his bread right into the middle of the hall. And nobody followed his example. The head-warder was in the hall, seated at his desk. He was quite unperturbed at Winslow's action. The head-warder knew the psychology of the convicts much better than Winslow did. The head-warder rose from behind his desk, very slowly, fixed his eye on Winslow, who was standing on the first offenders' landing, his arm still extended from having propelled the bread through the bars, and beckoned to Winslow with one finger. That was all. The head-warder didn't talk. He knew he had his man dead to rights.

Like someone hypnotised, Winslow followed the head-warder's beckoning finger; he came down from the landing and descended the iron stairs and made his way down to the grille gate leading into the hall. The head-warder unlocked the grille gate for Winslow, took his ticket off him, and had him charged before the Governor. It was all done very neatly, and without commotion. And Winslow got about two weeks' solitary confinement on rice water. If it had not been for the exceptional circumstances prevailing in the prison, the Governor said, he would have given Winslow lashes. And the convicts said they were glad that Winslow had been dealt with. And the old lags, with lots of previous convictions, said that the first offenders were getting more cheeky every day.

Nevertheless, for the next week or so, the food in the prison did show some sort of improvement.

And no more bread was cast into the hall thereafter. This wasn't so much on account of the fact that the convicts were supplied with more edible bread, but through a thoughtful step taken by the prison authorities. Many hundreds of square yards of steel-netting were ordered. All the convicts working in the fitters' and carpenters' shops were put on the job. And in next to no time the whole hall was closed in with steel-netting that you couldn't throw even mealie-porridge through.

The improvement in the quality of the food was as temporary

as it was slight. Regularly, at meal-times, a couple of dozen convicts would again be lined up in the hall, inviting the head-warder to partake of the repasts that they brought him in the tin-dixies. The head-warder's heart was perhaps touched by the solicitude of the convicts on his behalf: for he was getting over twenty dinners offered him every day – and for nothing. But if he appreciated this thoughtfulness on the part of the convicts, he certainly did not manifest his gratitude openly. Instead, some of the things he said to those convicts, every day, reached depths of obscenity that were remarkable even for a discipline head-warder.

The next thing that happened, therefore, was that there was a strike. The convicts marched out into the yard, one day after lunch, in accordance with long-established routine. They formed up in their various spans, and were checked out by the chief warder, and were ordered to advance to their respective workshops. But instead of marching out through the mortuary-gate, they stood firm. Just like that. There were a few cat-calls and a lot of slogans were shouted out about the porridge not being fit for a wart-hog to eat.

The chief warder ignored these observations. "Forward," he said again. But the leading span stood fast. The chief warder was not by temperament a man given to repeating himself. So the convicts went on standing, drawn up in long lines in the afternoon sun that shed its depressing yellow on the warders' uniforms and on the drab garb of the convicts. After a while a couple of parapet-guards were brought round; they were stationed on top of the wall with their rusty machine-guns trained into the yard. But nothing much happened. The convicts got tired of shouting after a while. And they got more tired of standing to attention in the afternoon sun. And the cat-calls grew feebler. And the statements to the effect that a hippopotamus couldn't drink the soup were uttered with less conviction.

That bit of a food-strike was not very successful, taken all round. Each convict felt, after a while, that by standing firm there, in the yard and not going to work in the shops, he wasn't spiting anybody. He was only making things unnecessarily uncomfortable for himself. The warders didn't mind. They were saved the trouble of accompanying the convicts into the workshops and seeing that they kept out of mischief. With all the convicts lined up in the yard, like that, it was easy to keep watch over the whole lot of them. But it was darned irksome for the convicts, this food-strike. The sun beat down on us unmercifully, and we felt that, lousy though it was to work in the stone-yard and such places, it was nevertheless streets better than standing to attention, stiffly, and in silence, with a lot of warders in position all round to time your every movement.

Consequently, when the Governor arrived in person, some hours later, and he announced (in a voice that he tried to make sound as much like a fog-horn as possible), that he would see into the rations position himself, his remarks were greeted with a fair amount of cheering. And so, when the chief warder repeated his command, but in the reverse direction – for he now bellowed, "About turn! Back to sections! Forward!" – not a convict but was pleased that the strike was at last over. It seemed a very long time, that couple of hours of standing to attention with the sun shining into your neck and the sweat pouring off your belly. And this in spite of the fact that *all* time, as Oscar Wilde took the trouble to point out, passes slowly when you are in prison.

Morally, this food-strike was a defeat for the convicts. Every convict in prison lost face through it. But in terms of practical politics the strike was a huge success. Because, apparently through the personal intervention of the Governor, the quality of the meals served up was much better than it had been for months. It was said that the Governor was anxious to keep the facts about the convicts' dissatisfaction over the food out of the newspapers. The Governor didn't want the prison to receive unfavourable Press publicity, the convicts said. They said that the Governor was afraid of the boob getting a bad name. I thought there was something rich about this, somehow: the thought of a prison Governor not wanting a prison to get a bad name. For fears that members of the general public, getting to hear these unfavourable reports about the place, would decide not to patronise the prison, likely. And without the prison's regular six hundred customers (in the form of convicts doing six months and over) there wouldn't be a job for the warders and the head-warders and the trades warders and the chief warder – and the Governor himself. That, at least, was what the convicts said.

Anyway, the food improved. And everybody was satisfied, except Blue-coat Verdamp. Because, as the days went by, his supporters dwindled. Even new first-offenders, who had arrived in the prison after the demonstrations were over, would know that some very important convict, whom they had not even met, had recently organised a protest demonstration that had resulted in the convicts being nowadays dished up with good food. There was no question of Alec the Ponce's head-ship. Even fellow-convicts who had been on bad terms with him for years, because he had stolen tobacco off them, or because he had had a stoppie dagga and had smoked it on his own, or for no other reason than that he was just a mongrel-bastard in any case – these convicts now began to show Alec the Ponce various small favours, like hauling out a tinder-box

quickly to light his cigarette for him, or ostentatiously remov-
ing his red-spotted handkerchief from his jacket-pocket on a
Saturday, and washing it for him, or saying, "Hallo, Alec," and
offering to help him with his wheel-barrow when he was
pushing it fully-loaded in the direction of the slag-heap.

You couldn't help noticing where Alec the Ponce stood
with the boys, in those early days after the food disturbances
had led to the convicts being served with better fare. You
couldn't help noticing the tone of deference with which he was
addressed. Everybody, too, now called him Alec; just plain
Alec, without the addition of that opprobrious descriptive
epithet. (For the word "ponce", in prison argot, means
"pimp", "procurer", "brothel-keeper", "whore-monger".) On
one occasion, even, a trades-warder in the boot-shop, in giving
him a job, called him by his name, Alec, instead of by his number. You could see, from that, that even warders were anxious
to get into his good books. Alec the Ponce had become a head,
all right: even though he was doing only four-and-a-half years.
He had blossomed out into a real old-time bigshot. He was a
prison-head par excellence and no argument.

This was gall to Blue-coat Verdamp. He wasn't used to
playing second-fiddle to a ponce, he said: to a man who would
take a whore's money off her – the money she had earned until
half-past three in the morning, mind you – and then sleep with
her.

Blue-coat Verdamp circulated some appalling stories about
Alec the Ponce's past. About some woman with both syphilis
and consumption who was so far advanced in disease as not to
be able to walk the streets any more; and then Alec would send
her about the streets in a ricksha, to pick up men, the ricksha-
boy transporting both the prostitute and her client to the door
of her room – when Alec would arrive from around the corner

to help lift the woman into the bed. And when this sick woman didn't earn enough, Alec the Ponce would thrash her with a piece of boot-sole nailed on to a length of plank.

Blue-coat Verdamp told all sorts of stories like that about his rival. All with the intention of discrediting him with the boys, of course. He also said that when Alec the Ponce got lashes, afterwards, for pimping, he howled so loud, with the cat-o'-nine-tails curving about his spine, that members of the public, walking past the prison at that hour, on their way to work, started running at the noise. Because Alec the Ponce's yells were so shrill and piercing that these people thought it was their train. And so they started running, thinking they were late for work. That was what Blue-coat Verdamp said. But his campaign of defamation came to nothing. Alec the Ponce was securely established as the prison-head. And, if anything, these libellous stories Blue-coat Verdamp spread about him served but to enhance his prestige.

And so Blue-coat Verdamp started getting desperate. Day by day he watched the food. He was going to make a complaint. Everybody knew it. And it was going to be a sensational kind of protest. That much we could all sense. Just let the food drop ever so slightly in quality, and at one stroke Blue-coat Verdamp was going to re-establish himself as the man every convict in the prison – and every warder, too, of course – was going to look up to. If the soup or the skilly or the bread or the porridge got bad again, just once, then Blue-coat Verdamp was going to express his dissatisfaction in a way that would make Alec the Ponce look like a first-offenders' section lavatory-cleaner. Just you wait.

That was what everybody in the prison was saying. And a queer atmosphere of tension began to hang over the lunch-periods. We would come in from work, day after day, and taste our carrot-soup. No, it was quite all right. Carrot-soup was, after all, only carrot-soup. And you couldn't squeal about it, as long as you could eat it. Carrot-soup was down on the diet-scale, and nothing could alter it. But then it had to taste like carrot-soup, and not like something else with which the convicts compared it. Then, one day, just when we had begun giving up hope of anything in the way of fire-works, the soup was noticeably off. No jokes. It was bad soup. Almost as bad as before the trouble started.

There is no describing that feeling of quivering ecstasy, of an almost masochistic sense of delight and fear and expectancy that took hold of the emotions of six hundred convicts that lunch-time, when they dipped their wooden spoons in their dixies and put their mouths to the soup . . . The warders were keyed up to almost the same pitch of excitement . . . Like a pale ghost that knowledge swept through the whole prison . . . The soup was crook. It was onkus. A yellow-bellied platypus couldn't drink it . . . And, yes, Blue-coat Verdamp had asked permission of his section-warder to proceed to the hall. That permission had been granted . . . The warders in their excitement forgot to lock the cells, which they were supposed to do after the last dixie of carrot-soup had been served . . . As many convicts and warders as could crowd on to the landings and the ends of the sections peered through the bars and wire-netting into the hall. In the penal section the crush was so great that the warders had to drive the convicts back with their batons . . . These warders wanted the best points of vantage for themselves . . .

Blue-coat Verdamp walked straight up to the head-warder, who was standing in front of his desk, trying to look non-chalant. But all the time he was eyeing Blue-coat Verdamp warily, out of the corner of his eye. If any man in that prison at that moment knew that there was trouble coming, that man was the head-warder in the hall. Carrying his dixie in front of him, and holding on to it with both hands, as though it was something very precious, Verdamp marched with a slow, almost trancelike gait, as though he had been smoking a large quantity of dagga. His face was very white. He approached the head-warder.

"Look what I have to put up with, sir," Blue-coat Verdamp announced.

"Food bad again, is it?" the head-warder queried, blandly. "Now, do you know what, if you give me a spoonful, I don't mind if I *do* taste some of it. Now, only a spoonful, mind."

That got Blue-coat Verdamp guessing, all right. It was a mighty clever move on the part of the head-warder. For the first time, in the history of the prison, it would mean that when a convict had come into the hall complaining about the food, the head-warder had tasted it. Yes, it was very good strategy on the part of the head-warder. But it was also his trump card. Blue-coat Verdamp paused irresolute. He had made history in the prison. The head-warder in the hall had offered to taste his carrot-soup. That would put Blue-coat Verdamp clear above Alec the Ponce as the chief convict head in the place. Let the head-warder drink a mouthful of that soup, in full view of all the convicts and warders looking on from the section landings, and Blue-coat Verdamp would emerge from the encounter as the hero of every convict in that prison, now and for many years to come.

The tension in the prison soared with each second that passed. Verdamp was quite close to the head-warder, now. He held out his dixie with one hand. With the other hand he extended his wooden spoon. The head-warder reached forward to take it.

"Drink a mouthful of that sewer water and drop dead!" a convict roared from a landing across the way. The head-warder turned round to face the convict who had shouted that remark. The head-warder was at his ease, now. He would deal with that convict. The whole thing was going to pass off without any irregularities taking place. It wouldn't be hard, either, to find that convict who had shouted. The section-warder would be able to help him in the search. The interruption had been most providential. He would make full use of that diversion.

And the moment the head-warder turned round – well, nobody could say very clearly, afterwards, how it all happened. It was so quick. And there was such confusion, with the spoon going one way, and the dixie of carrot-soup going another way, and discipline warders coming rushing in to the head-warder's assistance through four different grille gates . . . Nobody could say *exactly* what happened. But of the central feature of the event that occurred, the moment the head-warder's back was turned, there could be no doubt at all. And it was something that would be remembered for as long as there was a prison anywhere in the country. It was a story that would be passed on from one generation of warders and convicts to another. It was a legend that would grow only more gaudily coloured with the centuries.

For, with the historical remark, "This is where I takes a snout on you screws," Blue-coat Verdamp had let go a flying kick at the head-warder, the moment his back was turned, and had landed his convict boot square and solid up the head-warder's backside.

That's all there is to tell about it, of course. I can't hope to describe the pandemonium and the hullabaloo that followed, in the course of which Blue-coat Verdamp was knocked down and dragged out by half-a-dozen warders – whose numbers had increased to over a dozen by the time they had put him in irons and had locked him up in a solitary cell. Afterwards, when he was chucked into hospital, to have stitches put in his face and to have the more badly-crushed ribs on his right side removed, it was found that there was no need to have put Blue-coat Verdamp in leg-irons, because as the result of the doing he got on the way to the solitary cell he would never again, for the rest of his life, be able to walk without a crutch. But Blue-coat Verdamp had triumphed. He had made prison history. It was the first and the only time known to anybody at all who knew the inside life of prisons, that a convict had gone up to a warder – and a head-warder, on top of it – and had booted him up his behind. You can hit a warder with a pick-handle, to try and escape. You can even take a pot at a warder with a gun, if you can get hold of a gun, in order to try and make a break out of the boob. But to shoot a warder around with your boot, just to show your contempt for him – well, that was a different thing altogether. It was undreamt of. That you could try and overpower a warder and make a getaway: that was something everybody could understand and accept. And you'd get a couple of years for it. All right; and there would be no hard feelings. But what Blue-coat Verdamp had done, there in the hall, in the presence of the whole prison, letting a head-warder have it with his boot up his jack, just to show him how much he despised him – well, that was something utterly and for ever without precedent.

After Verdamp came out of hospital the head-warder made a case about it, of course, and the case was too serious for the Governor to try himself; so the matter had to come before a magistrate: whereby the whole story got into the newspapers, of course – the story that a convict had kicked a prison-warder because the food was bad. And Blue-coat Verdamp got two years' imprisonment with hard labour, which he would have to serve after he had completed his current sentence: and when that would be, God alone knew. And he had to be kept in irons for six months, and also in solitary on spare diet for six months – three days in, one day out. And the magistrate also granted him authority to have a crutch made in the carpenters' shop, to help him walk back to the section each time he came out of the solitary cell. And so everything was settled very nicely.

And for at least six months, what with all that publicity, the food in the prison was really good. We lived like kings. And if there was still some slime floating on top of the carrot-soup, every now and again, at all events it wasn't the kind of slime that made you feel all nauseated. And the irony of the whole situation, I often thought, during those months that followed in which the food was good – the irony of it was the fact that the man through whose energetic action this considerable improvement had been brought about could enjoy these new and palatable meals on only rare occasions: on only one day out of every four, in fact. Because during those other three days out of each four, and for a period of six months, in terms of his sentence, he was locked up in solitary confinement on spare diet – which in those days consisted of a pint or so of rice water.

And by the time Verdamp's solitary was up, i.e., at the expiration of six months, the prison food was, of course, back to its natural, putrid level.

But before the decline became noticeable, something rather funny happened. Because of the story having got into the newspapers of the convicts'·dissatisfaction with their rations, and particularly because of the unusual form in which one convict had manifested this general dissatisfaction. Head Office took cognisance of the matter. Accordingly an inspector of prisons was sent down to find out what sort of rations were in actual fact being served to the convicts. And the authorities were, as a matter of course, informed of his impending arrival. (I mean the prison authorities, including both those on the paid staff and those doing time.) There was a great deal of talk, in advance, about the fact that an inspector was coming down, on a certain day, to see for himself what the day's rations were like.

The inspector of prisons arrived. The prison kitchen rose to the occasion splendidly. We didn't get just carrot-soup, that day, but roast and two veg. And done to a turn. There was good, rich, thick gravy. You would have been lucky to get food as tasty as that in even the best class of hotel. The convicts lunched so sumptuously that next morning a large number reported sick: their starved digestive organs were unequal to the task of suddenly coping with a good meal.

That was the day the inspector of prisons paid his visit – well-advertised in advance – to enquire into the convicts' grievances about the way they were being fed.

A large number of convicts felt sore about the whole thing. "The inspector will go back and say we're eating better than the Prime Minister," they said, "And we'll get the name for being a mob of bleaters." And so on. But most of us didn't care a damn about any consideration other than the fact that we were sitting down to a feast such as had not been spread before us in years.

Then, to the amazement of the whole prison – for the news spread very rapidly through the prison, although only a few convicts witnessed the actual incident – it was learnt that two short-time convicts had gone down into the hall at lunch-time with the dixies containing their roast and two veg., and that they had demanded to be confronted with the inspector of prisons, and that they had said, "Even a pole-cat can't eat muck like this, sir. Will you please taste a mouthful and see?"

And the inspector of prisons had sampled their food, and he had turned purple with rage, and he had said, "God damn it! *I* don't get food like this every day. So this is the kind of food you complain about! I've never encountered such audacity in my life."

How was the inspector of prisons to guess that the head-warder in the hall, through the promise of getting them cushy jobs in the clothing store, had got those two short-term convicts to go up and make that complaint? For days afterwards the head-warder was observed to be wearing a fat sort of a smile on his face. It was an irritating smile: the head-warder in the hall seemed so darned pleased with himself . . . Smirking all over the place . . .

Chapter 8

AFTER I HAD SPENT about two-and-a-half years in the stone-yard I got promoted, the head trades-warder in the carpenters' shop having invited me to come and work in his shop. I want to make it clear that I had in no wise solicited this elevation. My rise out of the stone-yard into the carpenters' shop had been as unexpected as my original demotion from the printers' into the stone-yard. Needless to say, I was highly gratified at this mark of confidence reposed in me by the carpenters' head trades-warder. It showed that I was, with the years, becoming somebody of account in the prison, after all. I could never aspire to become a head, of course. I had no illusions about my ever being able to achieve to anything approaching spectacular success in my career of being a gaol-bird. I would never be looked up to as a dagga-king, for instance. And I would never have the status, even, of a convict who had four previous convictions. And if I did solitary from now on until doomsday, my opinion on any branch of art or literature or culture would still carry infinitely less authority than the considered judgment of a safe-blower serving the indeterminate sentence.

Nevertheless, the carpenters' head-warder, in getting me a change of labour into his shop, gracefully put the seal on a truth that was slowly beginning to enter my consciousness. And that was the fact that, in the prison, I had come to be accepted, both by convict and warder. This knowledge didn't give me a swelled head, however. I didn't get smug over it. At the same time, it would be ridiculous for me to pretend that I wasn't proud of this thing that had happened to me. I felt a warm glow, and I had a new and serene confidence in myself. I felt that the years I had spent in the prison had not been wasted. For I had, at last, arrived. A head-warder had, on his own, invited me into his shop, into a place where I would be sheltered from the wintry rains and the dust-storms of early summer and the mud that stretched ankle-deep over the stone-yard in the wet season, so that your boots would be clay-logged for months on end, and your pants and jacket stiff with mud.

Above all, the social stigma of being a member of the stone-pile gang was now lifted from me.

But, as I have made clear, I never allowed this change in my situation to disturb my sense of proportion. I recognised that I had my foot on a ladder that could lead to great and lofty attainment. I might be able to work my way up as high as head section-cleaner, for instance. Or I might even go as high as getting the job of helping to transport the weekly washing by handcart into the women's prison. I might even, through influence, be advanced to the position of looking after the master-tradesman's lavatory: a prized appointment on account of the many cigarette-ends scattered over the floor, every morning. But I also knew my own limitations. I would never attain to the eminence of being a *responsible* convict; somebody like Kak-kak, or Alec the Ponce, or the Bombay Duck, or Dagga Joe. I would never become a person to whose views on questions of the day both warder and convict would listen with polite attention. I was on the road to making a success of my career as a convict. That much I knew. The signs were there for all to read. But I would never attain to genuine *greatness* as a convict.

Nevertheless, there was one honour that, in my heart's secret recesses, I treasured as a possibility – as a distinction that, with a bit of luck, might just come my way if my progress continued without interruption for another few years: and that was that one day a warder, in addressing me (with a good lot of convicts around to hear it) would call me by my name and not by my number. Just once. It was an accolade that I had on various occasions seen conferred on other convicts who were well in the running for recognition as heads. To have a warder address you by your name instead of your number, conspicuously sewn on to your clothes, was an honour that a convict never forgot: even if it happened to him only once, during a long period of imprisonment.

And my secret ambition was that some day, some day when my star was in the ascendant, that honour would come to me, depraved mortal, also.

To be a convict and to have a warder look you in the face and call you by your name ... instead of looking at your pants or your shirt and calling you by your number ... or simply addressing you as "You!" or as "You bastard! ..."

If a warder says to you – and only once is enough – "Look here, Van der Merwe," or "Look here, Billy," or "Look here, Gumshoe," then, in that moment of being officially accepted as a human being, with a name or a nickname of your own, and not just a number – in that moment many years of prison degradation drop off you like soiled clothes.

2

Some months after I had been promoted to the carpenters' shop, Pym, the blue-coat whom I have mentioned before as having taken a fancy to me when I first started off as a hard labour convict, came out of penal. He was put to work in the book-binders'. So I saw a great deal of him. At exercise periods and so on. I saw far too much of him. He would wait for me in the mornings, so as to walk beside me to the yard where we fell in. Usually he would bring me little presents of food: a piece of bread with a chunk of fat on it, half an onion – delicacies like that. Because he was a blue-coat serving the indeterminate sentence, and had a long list of previous convictions, he had status in the prison and knew the ropes, so that he could get little extras in the way of food supplied to him sub rosa out of the kitchen or the stores. I was glad to have these little presents. But I was also embarrassed by his attentions. I was scared the warders and convicts would think I was homosexual, and that I was Pym's rabbit. It also made me feel unmanly, somehow, having this blue-coat hanging around me every chance he got, and smiling fatuously when he would meet me in the line, and handing me a cold potato.

Because he was doing the indeterminate sentence, the warders would allow him freedom of a sort that would not be permitted to short-timers or first offenders. When he came out of penal, Pym got himself put into the book-binders', where the work was light and from where he had plenty of opportunity of making contact with me. Almost every day he would ask the screw in the book-binders' to have a pair of scissors or a knife or some instrument sharpened in the carpenters' shop. And because he was doing the blue-coat, Pym would get permission to go to the carpenters' shop, even though the warder knew that having the knife, or whatever it was, ground and sharpened was only a pretext for him to come and talk to me while the job was being done. One day Pym came into the carpenters' with a saw that had to be sharpened and re-set. Another time he brought along a six-foot guillotine-blade that another convict had to help him to carry. And on each occasion Pym would come and stand by the bench where I was working; and he would talk to me and smile; and he would look very conspicuous in his blue-jacket; and I felt unutterably embarrassed, as I could sense what the convicts and warders were thinking.

And Pym also started arranging to come and see me in the first offenders' section at week-ends. He would come right up into my cage and chat to me during the quarter of an hour or so when we were unlocked. If the chief warder found him there he would have got solitary for leaving his own section. But the ordinary discipline warders that were on duty at the week-ends pretended not to notice Pym's presence in the first offenders' section, talking to me at the door of my cage.

All this made me very unhappy. I really didn't care for Pym very much. He was sort of more refined than the other blue-coats, but he had no originality of mind. And I felt that because he had made me presents of groceries and things when I had first started on my sentence, I was in some way indebted to him; and so I couldn't just turn unfriendly to him, now that I no longer needed his gifts.

Pym never made any homosexual proposals to me, except once, when he was very much under the influence of dagga. And I showed my revulsion so strongly that he never mentioned the subject again. But in his whole attitude he revealed his feelings for me. And I was not only distressed, but at times I also got terrified of him. I wasn't so much afraid of Pym as I was scared of this obsession that he had for me. He didn't have a friendly regard for me. He was not attracted to me by the qualities of my mind. He was simply infatuated with me, physically: it was a dreadful and unnatural infatuation. And I was frightened of it. And there was nothing I could do to free Pym of this obsession. What I felt for him was a mixture of fear, pity and hatred. For about a year after he came out of penal Pym's presence was a black shadow over my life in prison.

159

Round about the time when I had completed about three years of my sentence, a wave of culture-consciousness swept over the prison. It was very funny. Illiterate convicts started writing their autobiographies. And what a lot of lies they wrote, too: many of them brought their manuscripts to me to read. They mentioned nothing of the squalor of their lives outside the prison. To judge from their writings, even the lousiest illicit liquor-sellers were kings of commerce and tycoons of finance, outside. They all frequented the most fashionable night-clubs and hotels; i.e., the places that had been fashionable twenty years before – the last time many of them were outside. And they were dressed in morning-coats and spats and toppers. And when they went anywhere their chauffeurs would drive them in Rolls-Royces. And when they slept with a harlot they would toss her, as a parting gift, negligently, a platinum bracelet or a diamond necklace. (And, of course, it wouldn't be Big Dolly that they had been sleeping with. Oh, no. But some mining magnate's daughter. Or some near relative of the prison Governor. Or the daughter of a Judge . . . Every convict can tell you of at least one occasion on which he slept with the daughter of a Judge. And if it was a blue-coat telling you this, then he would be class-conscious about it, too: it wouldn't be just a circuit court Judge's daughter, but the daughter of a Judge of the Appellate Division.)

And they would have some snappy titles for the junk they wrote, too. Titles like "Twelve Times Innocently Convicted," or "My Days With the Corner House Millionaires" – "days" be it observed, and not, like now, "years" – or "Ruined Through Being Too Kind-hearted." There were lots of titles like that. But there was also a grim realism about the titles of some of these works of autobiography: like, "Put in Boob by a Nark," or "Twenty Years in Jug for Bugger-All", or "I Don't Care Now, Much," or "Why I Done Time," or "Cold Stone Jug".

But behind this urge on the part of the convicts to express themselves in prose autobiographies there were a number of other factors that I need not go into now. Suffice it to say that this ebullition of graphomania was only one manifestation of that yearning for culture and scholarship that, for a somewhat extensive period, infected the prison like a mediaeval plague.

The convicts started pestering the prison chaplains and the prison schoolmaster to arrange about getting correspondence courses for them. The subjects they wanted to study were of such incredible diversity that I feel my head swimming when I try to recall them.

For a while, ordinary conversation as between one convict and another took on an air of strangeness. They wouldn't talk about a new way of smuggling in dagga. Nor would they discuss the demerits of the detective who had put them behind bars – always a favourite subject with convicts, who would tell the story of their arrests over and over again, year in and year out, always getting the same enjoyment out of describing the johns who had pinched them as "motherless bastards" and "lousy —— mongrels". But conversation in the prison now began taking on a new kind of complexity. It was fashionable, at an encounter on exercise parade, for a convict to ask another as to how his studies were progressing.

As I have said, I don't want to go into any unnecessary detail about these correspondence courses: it would fill a whole book.

Nevertheless, it was not unusual to hear a convict say, "Well, I done finished my second paper for Doctor of Divinity. Post it Sunday night."

"Doctor of what?" his pal would enquire, "What's it any-way?"

"I dunno neither," the student would reply, "But that's the one I drawed a line under with my pencil on the list what the schoolmaster showed me."

The craze for culture and erudition reached its height, and its spiritual fulness, over the controversy about what was the difference between a quagga and a zebra. Nobody knew who started that teaser. But in no time everybody took it very seriously. It was regarded as a mark of educational attainment to be able to recite straight out, word perfect, just as it was in the dictionary, the definition of, respectively, a zebra and a quagga. If you asked somebody that question, and he said, "Well, I guess I just don't know. Some sort of striped giraffe, ain't it?" then you could feel very superior when you gave him the answer – if you knew it, of course.

There were several dictionaries in the prison, a couple being kept in the library, and one in the printers' shop, and one in the office where they censored the letters. And it was noticed, after a while, that in each of these dictionaries there was a piece cut out on a page having a lot of words beginning with Q, and also a piece removed from a page where the words began with Z.

Anyway, these are the definitions: *quagga*, n. one of the three species of striped wild horses, or more properly, wild asses, peculiar to Africa, of which the zebra is the type; and, *zebra*: n. a generic name given to the group of striped equidae, all of which are peculiar to the African continent, and this includes the Daauw or Burchell's zebra, the quagga and the true or mountain-zebra.

Those, at all events, were the two words that were missing from every dictionary in the prison after the controversy had started making real headway. And if you couldn't recite those two definitions off pat, no matter how you mispronounced the words, or how ignorant you were of their meaning, then you were regarded as a person with no educational attainments.

I remember a blue-coat once coming up to me, just after I had put on my brown moleskin jacket in the carpenters' shop, when the whistle for exercise fall-in had gone.

"Say." the blue-coat remarked to me, "You know the difference between a zebra and a quagga, don't you? I mean, there's hardly anybody in the prison as don't know the diff."

"No," I replied, "I don't know. A lot of chaps have asked me the same question. But I think it's just stupid. Who cares what the difference is, anyway?"

"Oh," the blue-coat said, and he looked quite sinister, "You don't know the difference? And you in the carpenters' shop. And a long-timer on top of it. Say, ain't you ashamed of yourself to be so ignorant?"

He was so worked up; there seemed even a veiled menace in his tone.

"No," I said, "I can't see that it's important to know just a couple of dictionary definitions. I really don't care what the difference is between a zebra and a kangaroo. And if I wanted to know, I could always go and look it up in a book, somewhere. But really, I am not interested —"

"You won't look it up in no book," the blue-coat pursued threateningly, "Not in this boob you won't. Them words is cut out of the dictionaries, see? And if you want to know the difference you got to keep it in your blooming head, see?"

He was getting nasty. So I thought I'd humour him.

"Well, do you know the difference, then?" I asked him.

The blue-coat snarled.

"Well, I'm doing the indeterminate sentence, ain't I?" he demanded trucently, "Of course, I knows the answer."

And he proceeded to recite the answer, all in one breath, and just like it was one word, "Quagga en oneo'th'threespecies-astripedwildorsesormoreproperlywildassespeculiart'Africaof-whichthezebra'sth'type."

"That's very good," I acknowledged, "You know what a quagga is, all right. Now say the zebra one."

The blue-coat shook his head. He looked apologetic.

"No," he answered, "I dunno that one yet. I only been studying three weeks, or maybe four weeks, but anyhow, less than a month. I studies in my peter every night. But I ain't got to zebra yet. All the boys in my cell is still doing quagga. Johnny Bay reads it out to us every night and we says it after him. When I knows zebra I'll come and let you know."

But I wasn't going to let this blue-coat off so easily.

"You've recited the whole thing," I said, "But now what does it mean?"

"Well, it's a quagga, ain't it?"

"Yes," I answered, "I know it's a quagga. But from what you've recited, all those words, if you were to see a quagga, would you know if it was a quagga?"

The blue-coat sneered.

"I stayed on a farm once, where there was quaggas," he announced, "And of course I knows a quagga when I sees one. A quagga is like a big buck, with stripes all over his backside, like he got lashes. That's a quagga. You can't fool me, you can't. You got to go and learn, that's what. You got no brains, that's that."

He had me licked, all right.

"But if you know what a quagga is," I pursued, weakly,

"What do you want to go and learn the definition out of a dictionary for?"

The blue-coat looked at me in scorn.

"That's eddication," he replied, "Ain't you never heard of eddication?"

While the fever for culture lasted, all sorts of queer things happened. Queer for the prison, that is. When you saw a group of convicts in earnest conversation, during that time, you would be wrong if you thought they were discussing the food question, or the low class of warder we were getting nowadays, or whether a certain young fellow really was a rabbit, or if he only acted like he was one. Instead, they would be discoursing on higher mathematics or Latin poetry of the Silver Age, or any other subject that sounded scholarly, and of which they had gathered the most amusing smatterings. Or they would be arguing about which was higher, a Ph.D. or an M.Sc. (Hons).

A man who had spent about fifteen years in prison went to the school-master, demanding to be enrolled in some correspondence college. The school-master was getting several applications of this nature every day.

"All right," the school-master said, "If you have sufficient gratuity to pay for the course you mentioned, I shall arrange to have you enrolled. But are you sure you will benefit from your studies? I mean, you want to take up B.A., don't you?"

"Yes, sir," the convict answered, "B.A. for a start, yes."

"But have you matriculated?" the school-master persisted, "I mean, you haven't passed standard six, have you? Have you ever passed any standard at all?"

"I dunno," the convict answered, truthfully.

"But then what is your standard of education?" the school-master continued patiently, "How much *do* you know, actually?"

"Well, I does know," the convict answered, with pardonable pride, "I does know the difference between a quagga and a zebra."

And he proceeded to recite those two definitions.

I couldn't reconcile this striving after academic laurels on the part of hard-labour convicts with my conceptions of reality. These convicts wanted a University education . . . when all the time they were in the finest University that there is. If they couldn't learn from being locked up in a prison, the grandest and most imposing and most ancient school that there is in the world, how could they hope to acquire any knowledge from an orthodox educational institution that could teach you only as far as B.A., and could confer on you no degree higher than a doctorate?

When I saw these misguided convicts immersed in their futile studies I couldn't help thinking along these lines: a convict with eight previous convictions – how much more knowledge has he not got of life than a University professor, passing his whole existence in the chalk-dust of the school-room and the lecture-theatre?

But after a while – a pretty long while, it seemed to me: but then all time in prison seems too long – this yearning for culture on the part of the convicts died away. The ponderous tomes that had lain about the cells for months were returned to the prison-library. It was discovered that the paper that these correspondence colleges roneoed their courses on was good for rolling cigarettes in. The writers of these and autobiographies and monographs and treatises wearied of their tasks. Life in the prison returned to normal. Dagga was once more king.

But there were one or two convicts who kept on studying,

year after year. I despised these convicts. Of what value did they think a degree acquired in prison would be to them, anyway? Only an illiterate man would spend his time in prison in study, and for that reason he would always remain illiterate, no matter how far he persisted with his studies. And he would also of necessity be a very stupid sort of a man. A man with no originality and with no sense of humour.

And of such a man would I ask, "What is the difference between a quagga and a zebra? ..."

A warder's pet. That's all he is.

4

During the fourth year of my imprisonment a very beautiful thing happened to me. I was working in the carpenters' shop, still. A bracket had to be fitted into a guard-post on the pavement in front of the prison. The head-warder sent me out to do the job. I went there escorted by a discipline warder and accompanied by another convict. It was a wonderful adventure. Even now, when I think of it, twenty years later, that old thrill comes back to me once more.

"Get your tools," the head-warder said to me, "And the timber for a bracket." To the discipline-warder he said, "Get your gun."

So we went out through the back-gate of the prison, the warder, the other convict and I. At the gate the warder got his revolver, which he slung over his shoulder on a strap. The other convict and I were searched. The outside warder opened the gate. Slowly, much too slowly, the gate creaked outward on its heavy iron hinges – and we saw the outside world.

Stout Cortez seeing the Pacific for the first time, from a peak on Darien ... All that sentimental rubbish. As though one piece of ocean could be different from any other piece of ocean ...

But in that moment of the gate swinging open very slowly, I saw the outside world again, after a period of four years.

"Forward," the discipline-warder said.

It sounded like the voice of Divinity talking. It meant we were going down that road which I had seen only once before, four years ago, and the sight of which had made my throat contract, because I had been under sentence of death, then, and as we had approached the gloomy exterior of the prison, and those forbidding-looking portals had reared up before me, it was with an unutterable despair that I had looked on that same road, for the last time.

We continued down that road, towards the front of the prison, where the guard-post was. Several times the discipline-warder had to shout at me to pick up my step. For every moment was ecstasy to me. I walked with an awful deliberation. I wanted to miss nothing. I wanted to go as slow as possible; those moments that we were outside the prison had to be stretched as long as days and hours and years; oh, we hadn't to go at more than a snail's pace. And I saw to it that we didn't. The warder could shout his head off. This dreadful ecstasy had to linger.

I have never in my life, before or since, beheld a scene as entrancing in its splendour as what I viewed from that dusty road, that was impregnated with a heady fragrance – that dusty red road skirting the prison. I have seen Funchal from the sea; I have walked those cobbled roads, green with young grass-blades like sprinkled confetti, and I couldn't see what there was in Madeira to thrill the tourists, who all said, "Oh," and "Oh," as though it was paradise. And I have seen middle-aged men standing in St. James' park and looking over the

168

bridge at the part of London other side Whitehall, with the early light of a summer morning on it: and I wondered what they saw in it. And the Paris boulevards, and in Brussels the Avenue Louise, and all sorts of other places and scenes – and among them, not least, the Hex River mountains from the train-window. I have seen lots of sights – since that day when I walked out of the back-gate of the prison, to go and put up that bracket at the guard-post. And all those sights have left me cold.

I don't think that even love has had for me the warmth and the beauty and the deep-drawn delight that came to me on that road, red with perfumed dust, skirting the prison. Love. Well, I was young. And I was in love with the whole world. And life had not yet been made sick for me through the poison of introspection. And so I walked slowly, in spite of the discipline warder's bellowings, in order to miss nothing, in order that this incredible joy that had come to me, suddenly and undeservedly, should fill my entire being, dropping rose-petals on the places where my shoulders were bruised.

It was a dream-world that I walked into. For four years I had been dreaming of a moment such as this was. I was outside. It was all *world*. I was walking along a road where free people walked, where members of the public walked – men and women and children: and above all, women. Sunlight and shadow and distance played queer tricks with my eyes. Because I had been confined within cramped walls for four years, my eyes were unable to accommodate themselves to the majesty of distance. To be able to see far away – fruit-trees a long way off, for instance, and a white-washed fence at the bottom of the road: all these things were very beautiful. They were invested with the magic of strangeness. I was in a painted world, queerly different from what I had expected the outside to be. I had so forgotten common things, that when I saw a couple of fowls in a back-yard I stopped and stared at them in an unspeakable joy.

For four years I had had only memories of what the world was really like. And what I saw now, distance and hues, and pale lights and patches of grass: they no longer corresponded to my ideas about them. They were quite different from my memories of them. And they were even more lovely than I had expected them to be.

For years I had dreamt of the world. I had tried, in the nights when I had lain awake, to recall that gaudy lost world that I had known up to the time when I was twenty. And I saw now that it was less brightly-coloured than I had pictured it to be. But I was not disappointed. On the contrary, this pallid reality was something infinitely more exquisite than my black and scarlet visionings of it had been.

We got to the guard-post much too soon. But before we entered it a woman and a girl came past: the wife and daughter of a warder. And they didn't look at us, of course. Because this was on the prison reserve, where they lived; and so they were used to seeing convicts.

But I stared at them, at this woman and girl. I couldn't look at them enough. I had to see them, and I had to remember. I had to remember everything about them, every detail of how they looked, and what they *felt* like. I had to remember everything about what that divine moment of their nearness did to my senses, and every single detail of their faces and their bodies and their eyes and their dresses, and the folds in their frocks, and the crinkles in the woman's legs, at the back of her knees, and the way their bodies swayed when they walked, and the way their light, summery dresses fluttered in the breeze when they walked. Above all, I had to remember that sublime impact on my soul, on my blood, of their having passed close to me. I must not forget that feeling of thick silence that was fragrant with the inside of them.

For I had to remember all that when I was locked up again. I had to treasure it all up; not a drop of it was to be spilt; and I did, as a matter of fact, succeed in keeping that memory vivid for at least a year after that – perhaps even longer.

The woman's dress was short. I hadn't expected that. How was I to know that women's fashions had undergone so much change during the four years in which I was shut away from the sound and sight of all women? And the little girl's frock was a washed-out sort of blue. I don't mean that the colour really was washed out, of course. It was only that I had expected the colours of materials to be more startling-hued than what they actually were. And I knew, instantly, that those really were the colours of the outside world, the colours of trees and the colours of dresses. I knew immediately that that girl wasn't wearing a faded dress. It was only that I had, during the years, come to imagine, in waking dreams of the outside world, that there was a brilliance about the things of living and the acts of living which was not really there.

But, of course, this pallor only enhanced the incredible miracle of the life that people lived. It made the mystery all the more refined. The glitter was all the more alluring, because it was subdued. Life was washed out, faded. So its attractiveness was a haunted thing. The outside world was deadly artistry.

After the bracket had been nailed into place, the convict who went with me having made holes in the wall with the cold chisel in the places where I showed him – mine being the higher-up job of hammering in the plugs and securing the bracket – we went back along the road we had come. But this time the convict who had come with me joined with the warder in making us hurry up. For it was getting on towards lunch-time, and my convict-colleague was hungry. He was only a short-timer; so in the walk between the guard-post and the back-gate of the prison there was little novelty for him.

But this time I didn't mind hurrying. I had already seen so much. I had a whole world of things to remember in the days to come. I had been allowed into fairy-land. I had thrilled to the earth and its beauty and its secrets. The faces and the figures of that woman and girl had not come up to my expectations in respect of the dark loveliness that I had come to associate with woman. But their beauty seemed all the more ethereal because it was not held fast in swift contours and vivid colouring. And their beauty had become all the more intangible because it made contact with my senses not as spirit but as clay. Paradise was so much nearer to me than the soil, during those years of my dreaming of the outside world. And what there was of clay in that girl and woman was a thing of far greater mystery to me than their quality of soul.

Reality was more trancelike than a vision, more breath-taking than any dream.

During the many months that followed, of my sojourning inside the walls, that saunter along the dusty road was a warm and luscious memory for me. It was an excursion into realms of gaudy adventure where my sight had been dazzled with shining fresh flowers and my ears had been filled with the sound of old gold. And life had been broken open like a ripe pomegranate, and tropical fronds had bent low in laughter, and spring had exulted in the stillness of young growth.

I had tiptoed down the corridors of ancient palaces, richly arrassed and niched with armorial bearings; my footsteps had wandered through sacred groves. And I would look at my feet, alone in my cell for many nights thereafter, and I would think that these feet, shod in these same boots, had walked down that road, once, and had got red dust on them, had walked in the same dust in which people of the outside world had walked, in which that girl and that woman had walked. And thinking like that I would not feel cut off from the world at all. For my boots were tangible proof that I was one with the earth and with life; proof – that any court of law would accept – that I belonged with people.

And, of course, the immediate effect of my adventure into Avalon was that my dreamings of the outside world became again exotic things of black and scarlet, heavy with perfumes, low-hung with the night. In my visionings the world outside the prison was invested with more vivid colours than ever before . . .

(Only the other day I passed that same spot again, by car. After an interval of twenty years. And the red road had been tarred. And I saw then that the whole distance we had walked, the distance from the back-gate to the guard-post, which still stood there on the corner – with the bracket still in place, no doubt, for I nailed it in solid – was less than a hundred yards.)

Chapter 9

AFTER MY WALK down that road, there seemed to be a spirit of liberation in the air of the prison. And I began to entertain queer hopes of being released shortly: of getting a special discharge – to use the official terminology. Now, any convict will tell you that when once a man starts getting hold of ideas like this, it is the beginning of insanity. And that was what began happening to me, of course. Although I held on to the hope, all the time, that the thing that was coming over me was only a form of neurosis, and not insanity at all. Oh, no, it hadn't to be insanity. I wrote to a friend outside and got him to send me in a number of books on psychology and psycho-therapeutics, and subjects like that. And wherever I encountered a passage in these books on the difference between neurosis and insanity, I would underline that passage, and I would read it over and over again, and memorise it. And I would cling to the contents of that piece of writing like a drowning person hangs on to a straw.

I searched through these books, furiously. And I came across several writers who maintained, very positively, that there was a clear line of demarcation between neurasthenia, on the one hand, and, on the other hand, the various forms of insanity, including schizophrenia, dementia praecox, depressive mania, idiocy and all other horrible-sounding mental conditions. Today, I don't know whether those psychotherapists were correct. Very possibly they were mistaken in holding those theories. But I do know that they saved my reason. And even at this great distance of time I am very grateful to them.

Over and over again I kept on reassuring myself. I said to myself that I had the authority of those eminent brain specialists, who all declared that my condition was only a matter of neurosis, and that it could never degenerate into insanity. This thing first came over me in chapel, one Sunday, while we were singing "Art thou weary, art thou languid?" with Pym standing next to me, singing out of the same hymn-book with me, just so that he could stand closer to me. And I hated Pym by then. I both feared and hated him. He had begun to haunt my dreams as he was haunting my waking hours. And I never cared, any more, what the other convicts and the warders thought of his association with me. I didn't care any more if they thought I was his rabbit, even. I was past caring. I only wanted to be free of him. I only wanted to be somewhere where his presence would not obtrude itself on my consciousness.

Anyway, I had been miserable like this for a long time. I bluffed myself that I was going to be discharged from prison shortly ... although, secretly, I knew also that I no longer cared. It was as though my whole life-force had been dissipated suddenly, as though, a little while back, all my desire for living had gone. And I believed I was going to be released from prison very soon. My recollection of that walk I had taken under escort to the guard-post no longer sustained me with its warmth. It seemed to have happened so very long ago. In another world, at another time ... And then in the chapel, on that Sunday morning, with Pym pressing against my shoulder as we sang, I saw a piece of blue sky looking at us through the bars of the chapel window. And on that piece of blue sky were etched, in black lines, the most terrible figures. And I was too horrified to look away, to look at the walls, to look at the floor. Because I knew that I would see those figures all over the place, etched in black lines, drawn in India ink across the whole universe. I have been haunted by those figures ever since. They have never gone. I can still see them, if I want to. I can see them on the white paper on which I am writing. They are there, now, at this very moment, twenty years later. Only, I have trained myself not to look. It took me many months of agony and terror to train myself to ignore these awful figures traced upon everything on which my eyes light.

Then, a few days later, when I was struggling with my terrors, when it had got so bad that I could still see these figures against the background of nothingness when I closed my eyes, then I heard one convict say something to another about "die lewe in die penal". I didn't know what he said. I wasn't interested. But that phrase, "die lewe in die penal." It frightened me. If he had said it in English, it wouldn't have got me like that, I am sure. "Life in the penal section" . . . no, I am certain that wouldn't have obsessed my mind.

I began to conceive of an awful "life" existing in the penal section, and afterwards in every section of the prison. I imagined this "life" as a vast, fat black serpent, trailing through all the corridors of the prison, through the walls and everything; filling the whole space between walls and roof, and the entire hall, and the whole prison; and this gigantic snake was alive and breathing, and it couldn't draw breath properly because it was so closely confined between walls and roof; and this was "die lewe" in the prison. The prison itself was a live thing, sweating and suffocating in its own immurement.

Then, for the first time, I became grateful for Pym's companionship. He was the only person in the prison to whom I could talk of my terrors. I dared not mention my frightening obsessions to anybody in the first offenders' section. I knew they would all be convinced, then, that I was mad. And they would avoid me, just as all the convicts always avoided any man who began to manifest signs of approaching insanity. And I knew that if the other convicts started avoiding me, because they thought I was going nuts, then I really would go mad. Because the thought of going mad inside the prison was a terrible thing. Every single convict in the place had a lurking fear of its happening to him. Because, periodically, a convict went mad. And you never knew whom it was going to happen to next. And there was nothing the warders could do about it. If the man was quiet and behaved himself, he just went on doing his time, as though he was normal. There were numbers of convicts like that in the prison. They were stark mad, some of them, and they suffered from all sorts of hallucinations: I don't want to mention any examples – because even at this distance of time they sound too frightening – and the sight of the quiet madmen in the place would make the sane convicts shudder; for every man in that prison had the fear, hidden away in the back of his mind, that some day, without his being able to do anything about it, his own reason would go, also.

When a convict got mad and violent the warders would lock him up in a solitary cell, where he could scream and dash himself about to his heart's content, and make himself filthy with his own ordure. The warders would also, at times, turn the hose-pipe on him. And this helped a lot, I think. Mostly, when a convict was in that state, he would die soon afterwards: which was the best thing for him, of course. Otherwise, if he kept up this raving form of insanity for a while, he would be transferred to the criminal lunatic asylum, from which he would never come out again. During the years in which I was in the prison, a considerable number of convicts had been transferred in this manner to the criminal lunatic asylum. The subject of insanity was never discussed in the prison. It was every convict's secret terror.

And so it was a relief for me to talk to Pym about my fears. And he said that my symptoms were nothing at all to worry about. He said it was quite natural for a man, after a while, to go a bit screwy in the head, especially if he had to spend a good number of years in a single cage, as I was doing. But Pym said that I hadn't to worry about it, much. I would certainly get over it, he assured me. If not in prison, then within the first few months of my being discharged from prison.

"Well, you know," I said to Pym, very confidentially, "I expect to be released shortly."

I saw a look of doubt come into Pym's eyes. I knew what that look meant. Pym knew that even if I got full first offender's remission I would still have a good number of years of my sentence to serve. And my saying to him that I thought I was going out shortly was one of the signs (according to convict lore) of coming insanity. I turned my face away. I felt sorry I had spoken. I remembered that brutal prison witticism:

"Old Alf says he's going out."

"He says that, does he? Well, he's going out all right. Out of his mind."

And it had to happen, of course, just at that particular time, that a convict did go mad. This sort of thing seemed to happen in bunches. Anyway, the convict's name was Krouse. He was a first offender. He was one of the cleaners in the section, and it had been noticed that he had got very quiet, lately: there was a suspicious sort of calmness about him. At least, that was what the other convicts said after he had started raving and the warders had locked him up in a solitary cell, through the peep-hole of which they were inserting the nozzle of a high-pressure hose-pipe at intervals.

And then a most awful thing occurred, too, a couple of nights after Krouse had been removed to the solitary cell. Some convict in one of the sections suddenly climbed up on to his stool and put his mouth as near to the bars as he could, and he started howling like a dog. Or a wolf. Or a hyena. But mostly, I think, it was like a dog. That was the first time something of that description had happened during the years I was in prison. So I got terrified: not at the man's doglike howling, but at what followed. Because, almost immediately afterwards, a convict in another cell took up that howl. Then another convict joined in. Before long there were several scores of convicts, standing on their stools and getting their mouth as near the bars as possible, emitting the weirdest sort of sounds into the night.

More and more convicts joined in. And yet more and more. It was a most contagious kind of thing. The noise each convict made, while it differed from the sounds emitted by his neighbour, nevertheless had one thing in common with this general howling, and that was that it had a warm animal ring: but it wasn't so much like an animal on heat as like an animal dying – or an animal smelling the stink of death. I know I didn't join in with this general howling. I pulled the blankets over my head and lay on the concrete floor of my cage and shivered. I was very frightened, that night.

Hours later, when the howling was still going on, spasmodically, throughout the prison, I noticed a pale refulgence at the barred cell-window which served three of the cages. I recognised that gleam. I had worked it out month after month. So I knew what that pale light was, now. In a few day's time it wouldn't show itself at all. Not through that barred aperture, anyway.

It was the full moon . . .

Next day, on our way to work, I spoke to the blue-coat Pym about the phenomenon of last night. Pym had been waiting for me, as usual, at the end of a narrow passage that served as the first offenders' exercise yard. This morning I was glad that Pym was waiting for me. I had nobody else that I could talk to about my growing mental fears. He had a sickly smile on his face and he had a little parcel in his hand: a carrot or a chunk of cold porridge that he had got hold of for me, somewhere. A little while ago I would have wanted to die of mortification, seeing Pym waiting for me there, with that fatuous smile on his clock, and holding out that little package. I would have felt that every convict and every warder within sight would have guessed that it all meant that I was Blue-coat Pym's rabbit. But this morning I didn't care. Pym was at least somebody I could talk to, about my terror of going mad.

"You weren't howling last night," I said to Pym, with an artificial pretence at being funny, "At least, I don't think I heard your voice. But tell me, the boys don't often get like that, do they?"

"How do you mean?" Pym enquired, "Like what do the boys get?"

"Don't kid to me," I said – and I grew very terrified all in a moment – "You know what I am talking about. The way dozens and dozens of the convicts, hundreds of them, I think, even, were howling last night."

"I don't know what you are talking about," Blue-coat Pym replied, very calmly, "I was awake nearly all night – thinking of you – and I didn't hear a thing."

I was aghast.

"Am I imagining it, then?" I asked, "Oh, God, I must really be going mad, then. It was the weirdest and most awful and most eerie wailing that I have heard in my life. I must have imagined it all. My mind must be going, all right. Didn't you hear it through your cell-window?"

"All that come in through my cell-window," Pym answered, "Was the moonshine. You know, my cell is on the other side of the block from you and when it is full moon it shines right on to my face, almost. Fifteen years ago a night head-warder had that window covered up with a piece of brown paper. That was when another con was sleeping in that cell. The night head-warder said that a convict had got no right to sleep with the full moon shining on his face, like he was enjoying himself outside. But that piece of brown paper got tore off long ago. It must be the full moon that has been making you feel queer. Howling? I ain't heard no howling."

"Don't say 'ain't'," I answered, trying to gain time and to think very hard. All right, I was going mad. That much was clear. But I didn't know I was as bad as all that: getting hallucinations, and especially such awful hallucinations of men howling into the night. Yes, it must be the effect of the full moon, after all.

Then I saw that Blue-coat Pym was laughing.

"Don't you worry about that, Pal," he said to me – and for about the first time since I had known him I felt no inner resentment at his calling me "Pal", a word that, in his uttering of it, he clothed in a subtlety of innuendo that had always grated on me – "It's this way, Pal. Of course, I heard them howlings. I would have been mad, all right, if I hadn't. And so would you. But you won't find any of the boys talk about it. Especially not them that howled. It don't happen very often. Not more than about once every five or seven years, I reckon. It only happened about three times, I think, during all the years I been in boob. The boys just sort of let themselves go. One bloke starts them off and then they all join in. And they dunno what they're doing. The first time I heard it, when I was a youngster, I got crap-scared. I thought as the whole boob was going mad, and me also."

"Don't say 'I thought *as*'," I corrected him again, trying to conceal my relief at his words.

"But the second time it didn't worry me any," Blue-coat Pym continued, "And I joined in, also, as far as I can remember. Howling away along with the other cons. And it happens each time with the full moon, I've noticed."

"Well you certainly had me in the blue funks," I said, "I really believed I was going out of my mind. When you said you hadn't heard a thing. God, you had me scared."

"But I been telling you, Pal," Pym went on, "There ain't – I mean, isn't – anything wrong with your brain at all. Every long-timer gets like you, after a few years: afraid he's going balmy. But you get over it. I think I got over the same thing about half-a-dozen times, all told. It never lasts more than about six months or a year, at a time."

And I could only think: Christ, if this has got to go on for another six days, never mind six months, or even six weeks, I'll be more than ready for the criminal lunatic asylum. What with these figures in front of my eyes all the time. And that monstrous conception of "the life in the penal" – that panting, sweating, writhing, suffocating fat serpent. And my awful, my abysmal terrors.

Then, after Pym had left me, and I had fallen into line in the span for the carpenters' shop, another fear began to obsess me. What if Pym had only said those things to comfort me? What if what he had said in the first place was true, and those convicts hadn't been howling at their barred windows? What if I had imagined it all, and Pym, merely in order to save my reason, had assured me that I really had heard all that howling?

What if Pym had now been telling me a lot of lies, just in order to comfort me? I was in a terrible state. I knew I couldn't say to Pym, next time I saw him, "Look here, man. Swear by your God's honour you are telling me the truth, and you're not simply trying to put my mind at rest. Swear that those convicts did howl, hundreds and hundreds of them." I knew he would swear to it, of course. What was the sacredness of an oath to him, he who had committed perjury in the dock hundreds of times, in his own defence, and had listened, as many times, to detectives committing perjury against him, in order to secure a conviction? Of course, and without any hesitation, Pym would swear that I had not been mistaken in what I had heard. And so I would never know whether that howling had been a reality, or whether I had imagined it. And Pym was right about another thing, also. No convict would talk about that night. I dared not go up to any convict and ask him, "Did you hear those weird noises, last night?" I dared not ask that question, for fear that the weird noises had existed only in my lunatic imagination. And no other convict would dare come and ask me that question, either, . . . in case I would think, in my turn, that he was going crazy . . . And the terror of insanity dominates the whole prison, asleep or awake.

One or two convicts spoke about the thing that had happened to Krouse, who was still locked up in solitary, with the hose being turned on him at intervals. The concensus of opinion was that he would either die shortly, or else get transferred to the criminal lunatic asylum. But nobody liked discussing his case at great length. Krouse, and the thing that had happened to him, seemed to touch us all too nearly.

"I expect he what-you-may-called himself too much," one man said, with a weak attempt at facetiousness.

"Or he must have smoked too much dagga," another man

commented, "I always says as a first offender shouldn't touch dagga."

"It wasn't the dagga he touched too much," the amateur wit repeated, "It was something else."

Needless to say, I felt none too happy at remarks of that nature, which were either addressed to me directly, or which I happened to overhear . . .

And during this time I found out what insanity was. I found it out through my own symptoms. I realised that insanity had nothing to do with the brain. The ancient Greeks were right. The seat of insanity was the stomach. When I got those mad feelings coming over me, at night, when I was locked up in my cage, and I could see those grotesque figures etched in black against the blackness of the steel walls, than I knew that my insanity wasn't coming out of my brain at all. Because my brain was working reasonably and logically, and I could think clearly. But that purple lunacy, that was like a handful of some slippery substance, was coming out of my stomach. That was where I was going mad: not in my head but in my stomach.

I wanted to go and see the doctor. But I was scared. I was sure that he would certify me. I hated Pym. It was a slow-burning, implacable hatred by now. But, paradoxically, he was the only man I could talk to, the only human being to whom I could pour out my fears. And I had no reservations about talking to Pym: not because I had any feelings of intimacy with him, but simply because I despised him. He had let me know that he was sexually attracted to me, and for that reason I despised him. And because of my contempt for him I didn't have to put on any sort of act with him. When I felt I was going mad, I could talk to him, and tell him things that I would never have dared confide to any other man in the prison, con-vict or warder or doctor, for fear he should consider me insane. And that was what I dreaded above all: the moment when a fellow-convict would detect that wild gleam that I was convinced shone in my eye; and he would say nothing, but he would sort of turn pale and walk away from me. Anyway, that was the paradox of my situation. I hated and despised Blue-coat Pym. And yet he was the only human being to whom I could turn in my distracted state.

One evening as we were marching back to the section, I overheard one convict ask of another why mules were sterile. And the other convict said, well, there had to be order in nature. You couldn't have too much bastardisation, or where would the world be? A human male and a female baboon could have intercourse, he explained ("Talking from experience?" – I wondered, idly, because my brain was sick) but they couldn't have any progeny. Otherwise it would be an impossible world, he said. What sort of a monstrous thing, for instance, wouldn't the progeny of a pig and a rooster be, he said, by way of example.

By the time I got back to the cell, after having overheard that last remark, my mind was in a state of fever. I was locked into my cage, and my mind revolved, over and over again, the import of that dreadful picture. A pig and a rooster would have sexual intercourse: and the offspring they would produce would be half pig, half rooster. A snout and a comb, and a curly tail and feathers. And pig's trotters with spurs. It was a nightmare thought that strangled me. And it wasn't so much a thought as a sensation. I could feel all this madness oozing up out of my belly. It was stomach insanity. All chaos had been let loose in my belly, and it was seeping through into my brain.

And this half rooster and half pig monstrosity – what if it went and mated with something else? With the progeny of the mating of an elephant and a frog, for instance, or the mating of a railway-engine with my jacket – my prison-jacket, with the number on, and all? Part frog and part jacket and part elephant's trunk and the tusks of a railway engine, and part – I was going mad. I tried to control my feelings. It was useless. My mind was in a whirl of horror and chaos. A frenzied world in which no single thing would have a brother or a sister or a father or a mother, because there would be nobody to look like him. And if a snake's tail hung down from where my head should be, and there were pieces of fish-scale and red brick in place of my hand, and I walked on one foot and two sticks and one wheel: what in the whole world would there be, in animate creation or in the inanimate realm, that I could fall in love with? What female would there be even remotely in my image?

These things were not so much thoughts as feelings. Horrible black feelings working their way up into my consciousness. I wanted to scream. I knew I was going to scream. But what was the use of screaming? It was very late at night. Nobody would hear me. Or the whole prison would hear me. The warders would come and lock me up next to Krouse. The terror mounted. I walked round and round my cage. It was even narrower, in the dark, here, in my state of dread, than it was in daylight.

When I took up the lid from my sanitary-pail and started hammering with it at the door of my cage, I don't know. But I must have been frantically pounding away at the steel for a long time. And I dimly remembered the convicts all round me swearing because they had been roused from their sleep. Anyway, I was still pounding at the door with that urine-pot lid when the door was unlocked by a warder, a young recruit. He stared at me, his eyes wide: I must either have been making a hell of a noise, or he had been smoking dagga. He looked at me as though he was in a daze. I felt better now that there was somebody to talk to. And I kept on saying to myself that I must be careful or I'd get certified. The young recruit must have thought to himself, also, that he had to be careful: seeing that he was dealing with a lunatic. I thought out carefully what I should say, and then I addressed the young recruit in English.

"I think I am suffering from some form of obsessional neurosis, sir," I said, "I think I require a sedative."

The young recruit stared at me for a long time without speaking. Then he said, very slowly, "Hoe sê jy?"

I burst out laughing. And then, when I heard my own laughter, the whole thing seemed even funnier, somehow. I stood in the doorway of the cage, laughing uproariously in the warder's face. Afterwards, when the young recruit was joined by two other warders, I was still laughing. I heard one of them say, "Daar het weer 'n ou mal geword." And another one said, "Vat hom af." And I was laughing more than ever when two warders caught hold of me, one by each arm – the third holding on to the scruff of my night-shirt from behind – and started conducting me down the corridor. And as we proceeded down the passage I heard convicts asking questions about me of one another.

"Who has done in his nut?" one convict asked (quite a creditable piece of prison-slang, incidentally, for a first offender who hadn't been inside very long).

"It's that long-timer down the end," came the answer.

"Better him than me," another convict said from inside his cell as I went past, "I'd sooner be dead than go to that criminal lunatic joint."

There were lots of eyes at the peep-holes of the convicts' cages when I was being escorted down the corridor.

In spite of the fears I had of being certified, I nevertheless knew that that laugh had done me a lot of good. It had driven the madness out of my stomach. The madness in my brain was nothing: I could control that any time: it was the black mass of slippery insanity that was a very foreign thing and that came out of my stomach that I feared. Let the black lunacy that came out of my stomach stay away, and I could make rings round a dozen doctors.

The warders wanted to take me to the solitary cells. But the young recruit said that he didn't know where the key was, and one of the other warders said he didn't know where the hose-pipe was. This was getting serious. I had to pull myself together.

"Look here," I said to the warders, in Afrikaans, "I'm not resisting."

"You'd better not try to resist, that's all," the young recruit said, menacingly, tightening his hold on the back of my blue-jean nightshirt and giving my neck a twist, "You'll come quiet if you know what's good for you."

"You won't resist much when we got that hose-pipe on you," the other warder said.

(He seems to have an obsession about the hose-pipe, I thought to myself. As bad as my obsession about that black snake.)

"Come on and no blasted nonsense," the third warder said, and he stamped his heel on my bare toes: for I was dressed only in that night-shirt when I had gone mad in the cage, and the warders hadn't given me a chance to dress. Not that I would have been able to dress in any case, then, the way I was laughing.

But I felt that things were now getting really serious. These three warders didn't know me. That was the worst about this thing having happened in the night, when the warders were all off duty, except for a few night-screws who hadn't been in the service long and didn't know the ropes. They didn't know me – which was a pity. But then they didn't know where to find the hose-pipe, either. And that was a blessing. The thought of the hose-pipe rather worried me. I hoped they would never find it. I didn't feel much like being drenched at that moment. It was cold enough, walking bare-footed on the cement floor and dressed only in a night-shirt.

But if only there was a warder about who had been in the service for some length of time, then I felt that I would be all right. As a long-timer who had already served a good number of years I was entitled, morally, to certain indulgencies. And the older warders knew that.

"Is Mr. Snyman on duty in the hospital section?" I asked one of the warders. I chanced my arm. It was a long shot. But my luck was dead in.

"Yes," the recruit conceded gruffly, "What about him?"

"Will you take me to him, please?" I asked, while they were trundling me across the hall: we had by this time successfully negotiated the iron stair-case and the going on my cold feet was rough.

"What do you want him for?" one of the warders asked, with a nasty tone in his voice, "Does he smuggle you in dagga? Is that what's wrong with you: is it too much dagga or is it the other thing?"

"I am a long-timer," I answered, just getting my foot out of the way again as the warder was once more bringing down his heel, "And I thought Mr. Snyman, whom I have known for about five years, might be able to help me."

They pulled me across the hall in silence. Then I got an idea.

"Mr. Snyman might be able to help you, also," I said, "He could tell you where the key to the solitary-cells is. And where to find the hose-pipe. He could turn the tap on for you, even. I hear the tap is hard to turn."

The warders looked at each other for a few moments in indecision. "All right," the young recruit said, his voice slightly less gruff, "We'll take you to Snyman. But no monkey-business, mind. Snyman will possibly also know where the key for the leg-irons is. And where they keep the brine to pickle the cat-o-nine-tails in."

And so they started marching me along to the door leading to the hospital section. Lest it should seem strange that the young recruit was displaying so much initiative in this little affair, I should like to explain that he was taking the lead, not by virtue of any seniority of service, but because he had been the first to get to the door when I was causing that commotion with the lid.

I had long stopped laughing. But my madness seemed to have left me. I was no longer depressed. Instead, the battle I was putting up now, with the warders, was giving me a new-found zest in life. I hoped this new feeling would last. One of the warders unlocked the door leading into the hospital section, and a few moments later we were in First-Class Warder Snyman's presence.

"What's all this?" Warder Snyman demanded.

"He's been banging his —— pot lid against the door of his cage and laughing," the recruit explained.

"Well, then, why didn't you bang him back?" Warder Snyman enquired, looking at me, "You mustn't take cheek from a convict, man. Bang him back on the head and see if he laughs then. Why didn't you just chuck the whole —— pot over him?"

The recruit scratched his head. Lord, he had never thought of that! Immediately he began to feel deferential towards Snyman. The recruit could see that you learnt a thing or two, of the ropes, through serving a long time as a warder. You knew how to act in an emergency. What a lot of bother he would have saved himself if he had acted like Snyman suggested ... I could sense all those thoughts going through the recruit's mind.

This was the moment I was waiting for.

"Meneer," I said to Warder Snyman, "They want to lock me up in solitary and turn the hose-pipe on me. So I asked these three officers to bring me to you. I have told them what a fine prison-officer you are, and I would also like to tell them now, in your presence, that the only reason why you weren't promoted head-warder long ago was through jealousy. And if you want the hose-pipe turned on me, sir, can I please put on my jacket first – so as to keep out the worst part of the water, sir?"

"Hose-pipe!" Warder Snyman exclaimed, "Nonsense! How can you turn a hose-pipe on a convict when he's not violent and screaming? Can't you see this man is a long-timer, and that he knows the ropes?"

The upshot of it was that I was locked up, not in the solitary cell, but in the observation cell, known as the bunk, which adjoined the hospital. I went in very happy. There was a mattress on the floor in the corner, and a lot of blankets. I crawled into bed. The luxury of a mattress, after all those years in which I had slept on the hard floor, was so thrilling that I felt I wanted to cry. I stretched myself out at full-length. Then I stretched out my arms. It was too wonderful. All this feeling of space. Nowhere did my toes or my hands touch the walls of the cell. It was heavenly, here in the observation-cell. It was so fine, in fact, that I couldn't get to sleep. The mattress was a luxury and a novelty: but I couldn't just suddenly re-acquire the habit of falling asleep on something as soft and resilient as a mattress flung on the floor. It took me a very long time to get to sleep.

And when I woke up in the morning I found that I had rolled off the mattress and that I had had a very comfortable sleep on the hard floor that I was used to.

I wasn't expected to go to work next day. There was a peep-hole in the door of the observation-cell, and periodically I would see an eye staring at me through the glass. I wondered whether I should pull faces.

But I was really comfortable in that observation-cell, other-wise known as the bunk. My foot was a bit painful, of course. Because, when the three warders had brought me as far as the bunk, on First-Class Warder Snyman's instructions, the warder who had earlier on trodden on my foot succeeded, at our final leave-taking, when I was momentarily off my guard, in bringing his booted heel down heavily on to the central part of my in-step, and with such good effect that several of my metatarsal bones got dislocated. So I was limping for a while. But other-wise I was happy. I stayed in that observation-cell for three days; and the food was excellent: I was on the same diet as the rest of the hospital patients. And after a couple of days I got myself used, even, to sleeping on a mattress.

And then, just when I was getting happy, and it seemed that all those mental fears from which I was suffering were in-substantial phantasmagoria – things that couldn't possibly scare any person with a normal adult brain – then it was, suddenly, that I found my fears coming back with redoubled force. They came out of my stomach, those terrors. That slippery black mass that was in my guts began to let loose, once more, those hideous feelings that fastened themselves on to the back of my neck, so that my head became hot, like it was molten glass, and that clarity that was part of my normal rat onal functionings became dissipated. It was awful. I don't know how it came about. I only knew that suddenly, out of the blue, all those horrors came and re-attached themselves to my mind, that had got made strangely serene through the success of the battle I had put up, first with the three warders and thereafter with Snyman.

I really was in a state of animal despair, then ... I knew I would be brought before the doctor, shortly. And I knew that I had no weapons left in my rusty old intellectual armoury with which I could defend myself.

I had received a note from Blue-coat Pym just about that time, when I started going mad all over again. Somehow, in my unconscious mind I identified Blue-coat Pym and his homosexual attachment to me as the cause of my insanity. But I only *felt* like that about it. I couldn't find any links, in actuality, between these two sets of facts: one, the set of facts associated with my going mad; and, two, the set of facts associated with Blue-coat Pym having a sexual infatuation for my person.

Anyway, I had been in the bunk for two days when a convict, who had the job of assistant orderly, passed a note in to me, along with my soup. The convict-orderly winked at me when he passed me that note. And I was used to getting that sort of wink – just that exact sort of wink – from section-cleaners who had passed me notes from Blue-coat Pym. And when I saw the writing on the piece of brown paper in which the note was wrapped, then I knew that it was from Pym. It was with the most complete sense of horror, and in the most abject fear, and loathing, also, and hatred for Pym, that I opened that note. And its contents were just what I had expected – just what I was used to.

He started off by calling me his Blue-Eyed Pal. (I can't possibly be expected to remember all the rest of the endearments: certainly not over this distance of time, over the distance of a quarter of a century). And he told me that I was to cheer up. And he said that the boys had faith in me, and that they all knew it was only a temporary break-down, and that I would see my time through like a man, and that I wouldn't get certified for the Criminal Lunatic Asylum. He said that he had that same faith in me. And he said that if there was any question of my going mad, which he knew there wasn't, then he would himself play-act insanity, in order to ensure of his also being sent to the Criminal Lunatic Asylum. Wherever I went he would go, also, he assured me. Furthermore, he wished to inform me that the fact that I had suddenly been removed to the observation-cell had imparted so severe a shock to his sensibilities, that he was *really* afraid of going mad.

He wrote all that, in his note, and a whole lot of slush besides.

And I was horrified. It seemed dreadful to me, this threat of Pym's. Even in the realm of insanity he would still be my hated shadow. Nowhere in the whole world would there be a nook, a corner, a cave, where I would be safe from his serpent pursuit. But a serpent does not pursue anything, I reflected. No, I answered myself: but Pym does. The serpent coiled throughout the cells and sections of the prison. That must be Pym, I thought. Pym. "Die lewe in die penal." Well, did I not first meet Pym when he was in the penal? It all sounded very convincing. But where did it lead me? To no place at all. I was going mad in this prison. And I was haunted by the terror of going mad. And every convict in the prison was in the same position – was obsessed by the same fears. Pym or no Pym, the fear of going insane within the walls of the prison was uppermost in every convict's mind. And I realised that that was the thing I had been afraid of from the moment I had entered the prison, from the moment in which I had been told that I had ten years to serve. It was a fear that I had not at any time, until now, admitted to myself consciously. But it was the one fear that had lurked underneath the conscious things in my mind from that hour until now.

I had not minded hardship. Confinement. Degradation. The humiliation of being bullied around by warders. Of being booted up or down stairs. These were comparatively innocuous things. What had made the iron of the bars and the steel of the doors and the granite of the walls penetrate into my innermost soul was the one fear that before I left the prison I would be a lunatic. And that fear had caught up with me now . . .

At the end of the third day of my stay in the bunk, with eyes staring at me through the peep-hole in the door at intervals, I was brought before the doctor. I was still clad, neatly if not elegantly, in my blue-jean night-shirt. That was all I had on. Nothing else.

And I am afraid that, from the medical point of view, my interview with the doctor was rather by way of being a farce. I mean, my black-slippery guts-madness was leaving me alone for a bit, enabling me to fence with the doctor with sufficient skill to keep me out of the criminal lunatic asylum. I had very little difficulty in convincing the doctor of my sanity.

The doctor gave me a whole lot of little animals – painted clay models of horses and cows and giraffes and dogs and things – to sort into their various groups. I did that easily, with my left hand, while talking to the doctor about other things. I purposely kept on talking, very quickly, about other matters . . . I don't remember what the doctor answered, or whether he answered at all. I wasn't interested. I sorted those little clay models of pigs and antelopes into their classes, and I was all the time trying to keep my mind away from the one fear that haunted me.

195

What if these little clay animals should start breeding outside their species? The pig with the buck, the dog with the horse? All that over again? I was fighting down that horror, all the time I was talking to the doctor. And I was doing the sorting easily, with my left hand.

But I was overcome with horror, all the time, at the thought of the monstrous progeny that would result from the various animals mating out of their species, and I didn't want the doctor to know of the terrors in my brain, and so I talked, very quickly, of all sorts of other things.

The next test the doctor gave me was even simpler. Something to do with little coloured cubes and squares and cylinders and circles, and things. And I could have done it blind-folded. Because in these little geometrical shapes there was nothing to be scared of. Let a circle mate with a cube or even with a rhombic dodecahedron, and nobody would be any the worse for it. There would be no harm done. You would be able to work out the result, exactly, in terms of solid geometry ... I started feeling so confident, I wanted to start setting the doctor a couple of tests, simple ones ... Instead, the doctor gave me a few more problems to work out. I did them so quick, his eyes nearly popped out of his head. I saw I had come out of his investigation of my mental condition with colours flying. So I got daring.

"Say, doc," I began, airily, "I am sorry, sir, I mean, doctor, I believe that I am going to be discharged from this prison pretty soon. Yes, sir, one of these days I am going to walk out of that front gate a free man."

I could see that the doctor knew that one, also. He had also heard that story, that it was a sign of insanity when a man with still a long stretch of time ahead of him began imagining that he was going to be released. You could see it a mile off, the suspicion that crept into the doctor's eye when I made that remark.

"Oh, I see," the doctor said, in what he no doubt thought were very disarming tones. "Has your sentence almost expired?"

I burst out laughing.

"You thought you had me there, didn't you, doc, I mean quack – oh, I mean doctor," I spluttered, "You really thought you'd got me, didn't you? Well, I only said that because I wanted to pull your leg a little bit . . . I hope you don't mind, doctor? No ill-feelings, really. I had heard that it was supposed to be a sign of approaching insanity when a convict starts imagining that he is being released, when he has still got years and years to work through. I hope you don't mind that bit of fun, doctor?"

The doctor smiled. He became human. I had won him.

"I know you convicts call me a quack and a horse-doctor, and all that sort of thing behind my back," he answered. "But I think I can tell pretty well what's what. You can't have been a prison doctor for close on to twenty years, as I have been, without learning a good bit about life. And about people. And about when a man is mad and when he isn't. I would like to write a book of reminiscences, some day."

My brain started working destructively again. If you had any sort of sense or gumption at all, I thought to myself (thinking of the doctor) then you wouldn't have remained a prison-quack for twenty years. Not by a long chalk you wouldn't have. The boys are quite right to call you a horse-doctor . . .

Then, my brain still active in a spirit of perversity, I leant forward, without being able to restrain myself – although all my sounder instincts bade me desist – and with an air of imparting something ever so confidential I asserted, "You

know, doctor, joking apart, I really believe that I *am* going to
be discharged from prison shortly. I don't know why. I have
got no reason for thinking it. I can only say that, as the saying
goes, I feel it in my waters."

This time I had him, of course. He didn't know where he
was with me. He looked at me in frank puzzlement . . . It was
some imp or irresponsibility inside me. I knew I was mad, and
I had managed to convince the doctor that I was sane. Now
that spirit of nonsense for its own sake, that has ever been the
bane of my life, decided that I was finally to leave the doctor
in doubt as to the truth of my mental condition, with the result
that I brought along, from right the other side of hell, that
friendly statement about my going to be discharged from prison
shortly.

Anyway, the upshot of the whole thing was that I remained
in the prison hospital for about three months. Sometimes I was
in the observation-cell, the bunk. At other times I was in
hospital in the capacity of a temporary convict-orderly, when
my duties consisted in helping to look after the bed-patients.
But I had got the doctor so muddled, with my bit of playfulness,
that three months were to pass before he finally came to the
conclusion that I was sufficiently normal, mentally, to be allowed to go back to the section.

And I enjoyed this period of my imprisonment: whether I
was locked up in the bunk, under medical observation, or
whether I wandered about the wards as a temporary convict-
orderly. I was kept on hospital food; and I had leisure for
reading; and I had a soft mattress to sleep on; and I could chat
with the ward-patients.

I made friends with a safe-blower who had worked his way
into hospital by some subtle, underhand means. His name was
Parkins. He was doing time under an alias. He was regarded as

the finest safe-blower in the country. And he was spending all his time in the prison-hospital, leading a life of ease and luxury. He told me how he did it, one day.

"It's easy, man," Parkins said to me, "And I can see as how you are learning the ropes, also, for swinging the lead on these bastards. All I have done, so far, is play mad. They copped me beating the urine in my —— pot into foam, one morning, like it was an egg-flip. I was beating my urine up with my spoon, just to make them think I was mad. And so I got bunged into the observation-cell. That was just what I wanted, of course. And then they brings the quack along, and I kids to him, also. And I been here ever since. I been living like a lord. The quack thinks as I am stone balmy, but not mad enough to be sent to the Criminal Lunatic Asylum. And so he keeps me here. I got him real interested in me case. He really thinks as I'm half-way to being nuts. You take my tip and do the same thing. Act up as if you're screwy. But not too much, mind. Just enough to get the old horse-doctor really interested in you. If you overdoes it, before you know where you are you are all certified for the Criminal Lunatic."

I looked at Parkins, the safe-blower, with a degree of respect.

"Have you been here, like that, all the time, swinging the lead?" I asked him, "Have you been treated as a hospital patient during all these years —"

"Five and a half years," Safe-Blower Parkins asserted with pride.

"And you've been swinging the lead all the time?" I continued, "And the quack has never tumbled to it? And all this time you've been absolutely sane?"

"Absolutely," Parkins answered, "And it's dead simple, man. You try it, also. Every time I sees the quack, I tells him the same story, about a million and a half pounds, all in Kruger sovereigns, as I have got hidden in the old Robinson dump. Then when the quack starts believing that maybe there is a certain amount of truth in that story, and he asks can't I perhaps draw up a little plan for him, to show the location of the treasure – not as he wants to dig it up, of course, but just for general interest – then I springs it on him that I also got fifteen million pounds all saved up in the Bank of England. That gets him, every time. He don't know where he is with me, man. You try it on him also. You pull the quack's leg the right way. Kid to him like I have told you, and you won't go to the section no more. He'll keep you here under observation for the rest of your time."

I was very much interested in the advice that Parkins, the nationally-famous safe-blower, who was doing all his time in the hospital, had to impart to me. So I broached the subject to him again, I felt that he had good advice to give me. I reasoned that a man couldn't be as good a safe-blower as Parkins and not know a thing or two about life.

"Is that all you got to do?" I asked him, "Have you just got to kid that you are balmy? Without going too far – like getting violent? And then are you sweet with the doctor for doing the rest of your time in hospital?"

"That's all it is," Parkins assured me, "You got to be sane, like I am – dead sane – and then you got to bluff just a bit that you're mad. And then the doctor doesn't know where the hell he is."

I reflected on Parkin's advice. Strangely enough, it seemed to me that this was the exact course that I was myself pursuing, unconsciously, and just out of perversity, and it seemed that my line was working with the quack. And then Parkins made a remark that seemed to cut the ground out from under my feet in one hit.

"Of course," he explained, with an air of great secrecy, "Of course, them Kruger sovereigns is all collected together under the sand of the Robinson mine-dump. But the doctor don't know as it is all true. The moment I gets out from here I'm going to hire a dozen kafirs with spades and I'm going to dig up that treasure. The doctor doesn't know that what I tells him isn't really a lot of lies. But that story about me having fifteen million in the Bank of England – that I just made up to kid him, just he should think I was off my rocker. Can you imagine a safe-blower like me having fifteen million pounds saved up in the Bank of England?

"But I taken a fancy to you. I dunno why that is. Sometimes I takes a fancy to a young fellow, when I can't get a woman. And I'll tell you what I'll do for you. Got a blank cheque form on you? No? Oh, that's a pity. Because I'd give you a cheque for half a million pounds right now. Only because I like you, mind. That head-warder in the hall, now, I wouldn't give him as much as a sausage. But do you know what the Kruger sovereigns I got in the Robinson dump are worth today? A tidy bit, I'd imagine. You ain't got a cigarette on you, have you?"

I walked away from him, then. And I know that my footsteps were unsteady . . .

I remained in hospital for three months. Sometimes I was in the observation-cell, and at other times I was allowed to wander about the wards, helping to attend to the patients. But I had learnt one thing. And that was that I was mad, stone mad. And that all the other people in the world were mad, also. And I learnt that what I had to do was to play-act sane. And I am still doing that same thing. I am still play-acting sane: it has come easy to me, with the years. And I have learnt now how not to see these horrid figures etched in black lines on the paper, as I write. And I have learnt how to think of other things very quickly when those fears come up into my head from that slippery black mass moving about in my belly. And I feel very confident, nowadays. I know I can lick my insanity every time. Or nearly every time.

What also helped me a lot, when I was in hospital, was the fact that I suddenly stopped getting love-letters from Pym, the blue-coat. The cessation in Pym's correspondence made me very happy. I felt he had forgotten all about me, and that he was no longer a menace to my peace of mind. I hoped it meant that he had found some other young fellow on whom he could lavish his homosexual affections. Because, in the prison-hospital, I was cut off from the rest of the prison. I didn't know what was going on in the workshops or the sections.

But after I had got discharged from the hospital, and I went back into my convict garb, and I returned to my cage in the first offenders' section, then I learnt why I had suddenly stopped getting notes from Pym, the blue-coat.

Pym had started raving, one night, in his cell. And he had foamed at the mouth, and had been very violent. And three warders had taken him out and had locked him up in solitary. And he had bitten a warder's hand right through. And after he had been subjected to the hose-pipe treatment for a couple of weeks, without showing any signs of returning to normal, Pym, the blue-coat, had been carted off to the Criminal Lunatic Asylum.

Chapter 10

I WAS BACK in the section, back to the cells and the workshops and the daily grind. The going was rather terrible. With my sanity in the balance, as I knew it to be, I went through hell. I am not going to try to explain what I suffered. Every moment, almost, I thought I would go right off my rocker and start raving. At other times I was obsessed with the fear of a warder or a fellow-convict spotting the madness in my eyes, and giving me a wide berth, in consequence: and I knew that whoever spotted my insanity would pass on that information to somebody else, and so on. And then, no matter how hard I played sane, I would be classed as a lunatic. And every time, at night, when the steel door was banged shut on me by the warder, and I heard the key grate in the lock, then my head would start spinning, and I would crawl round and round on the concrete floor of my cage, round and round, with great difficulty, on my hands and knees, because of the narrowness of the walls of the cage. I would crawl round and round, like that, until I would drop down from exhaustion. And yet I had a strange cunning, with all this. I would time myself. The warders, coming along the corridor at hourly intervals and looking in through one peep-hole after another, would never catch me out crawling round and round the steel cage. Whenever I sensed that the warder was almost due I would grab up a book, any sort of a book, and I would sit down on the floor and pretend to read. And as soon as I had seen the warder's eye appear at the peep-hole I would resume my crawling. On hands and knees, round and round. I got very good at this crawling, after a while. I crawled very noiselessly. And I had got the trick of pulling in my buttocks, in just the right way, at each corner, so that I just rubbed my backside against the steel partitionings each time I made a full turn.

One night the warder came back again, unexpectedly, after he had looked in once and had seen me sitting on the floor, pretending to read.

And so he caught me crawling, like that. And for a couple of moments after he had shouted out and asked me what I was doing, I was terrified. I thought he had collared me dead to rights, now, and the whole thing would come out and it would be me booked for the bughouse.

But I didn't lose my head. And I answered quickly.

"I am looking for my ticket-pocket, sir," I replied, getting up from the floor and going to talk to the warder through the peep-hole.

"But what you want your bleeding ticket-pocket for this time of the night?" the warder demanded.

"The ticket-pocket came off my jacket, sir," I explained, "and so I started looking for it."

"That's a funny thing to do," the warder said, and he sounded nonplussed, "Crawling around on your hands and knees like you're mad, looking for your ticket-pocket."

"It wasn't the ticket-*pocket* I wanted, actually," I said to the warder, "What I actually was after was the ticket inside the ticket-pocket. I wanted to work out how much time I still got to do."

My brain was working very fast. I felt I could outwit a dozen warders, and also the whole world. Lord, they'd never tumble to it that I was mad! I had all sorts of illusions of grandeur, suddenly. Let them all come! I could do the most ridiculous things, and I could get away with it. I had a brain that could think out the most plausible excuses for the blackest kind of insanity that came out of my mad guts.

The warder looked at the card on my cage-door. He read out my name, crime, sentence, date of conviction, date of discharge, prison number, religion and workshop.

"Well, you still got quite a few years to do," he announced, after having, apparently, done a bit of mental arithmetic.

"Yes, sir," I answered, "But I wanted to calculate it exactly. You see, I get a quarter off, for first offender's good conduct remission, and six months special mitigation for the Flag Bill (we all got that off you know, sir), and two months off because of the Prince of Wales's visit, and another —"

"You bastards get far too much time off," the warder interrupted me curtly, "The authorities must be mad to give you time off like that."

"Yes, sir," I agreed with the warder, promptly. I was very glad of what he had said.

He had said that the authorities were mad. That gave me more confidence than ever. I didn't feel so lonely and cut off from the rest of mankind, in my insanity. Here were the authorities also mad. I had the warder's word for it. I had a sudden, vivid picture of the authorities also crawling round and round on the floors of their bedrooms. It cheered me up no end, that ridiculous thought of the authorities also having to be careful of the way they manipulated their buttocks round the corners . . .

2

I was restive. I couldn't go back to the carpenters' shop. So I got myself a change of labour into the mat-shop, and from there to the brush-shop, and from there to the book-binders'. I got these changes of labour through influence. For I was a

long-timer who had also done a good long stretch, and so I was
regarded as being a bit of a head. So I was allowed changes of
labour which would not have been permitted me when I first
started off on my prison sentence. I had come a long way since
those early days when they could chivvy me around from pillar
to post, just like they wanted to. I remembered my humiliation,
at the commencement of my imprisonment, when I was
chucked right into the stone-yard from the printers' shop, and
with no explanation at all. That seemed to have happened in
another life, almost. It seemed so long ago. Well, it was a long
time ago, of course . . .

3

There isn't a single convict in the prison that hasn't got the
hope, some time or other of getting a special discharge from
the Department of Justice. The result is that the Minister of
Justice is inundated with petitions from convicts inside the
prison. I reckon that the Department must get thousands of
petitions every year. Millions, even, maybe. I have mentioned
the carpenters' shop, the stone-yard, the book-binders, the
tailor-shop, the brush-makers: well, the prison has got quite a
number of flourishing industries. But the most important
industry of all is that conducted by the convicts themselves. It
is the great prison industry of drawing up and forwarding
petitions for mitigation of sentence or discharge to the Department of Justice. I believe that I must have drawn up at least
a hundred petitions for various convicts labouring under the
pathetic delusion that these petitions got read at all. At the
same time, I also drew up a few petitions on my own behalf . . .
So foolish is the human mind.

One man told me that he had been sentenced to six lashes
and two years for incest. He didn't mind the two years so much.

But he did feel upset at the thought of those lashes. He had not yet got the lashes. That part of his sentence had still to be confirmed by the Minister of Justice. It usually took about a month for this confirmation to come through. So he requested me, in the meantime, while there was yet time, to draw up a petition on his behalf, couched in the strongest possible terms, asking the Minister of Justice to remit the lashes.

I did my best. I spent a whole night in my cage with pen and ink and paper (it took my mind off the necessity for crawling around on the cement floor) and I turned out a wonderful job, complete with elaborate scroll-work, and Greetings, and Whereas. If I had had some red ink as well, the Minister of Justice would have been able to frame this petition as an illuminated address. I used every possible argument I could think of: the petitioner's good character in the past; the esteem in which he was held in the community in which he resided; the fact that he had been exposed to temptation, and that two years was, after all, adequate punishment; and how much lashes hurt. I also mentioned the fact that, if he had those lashes inflicted on him, petitioner's buttocks would be marked with the stripes for life; he would feel very self-conscious about his wife seeing those marks. Then, introducing a personal note, I asked the Minister of Justice how *he* would like to get six lashes – and how *he* would feel at having to expose a striped behind to his wife's gaze.

The petition was handed in. About six weeks later I saw that same convict again – the man on whose behalf I had drawn up the petition. He was pushing a wheel-barrow. "I got those lashes," he announced sullenly, when he passed me.

He needn't have told me that. I could see it from the way he was still limping.

Anyway, I wrote lots of petitions for convicts who hoped

to get some time off. They had confidence in me. The longer I did, the more their confidence in me grew. They looked on me as a long-timer who had already completed a pretty substantial stretch. And so they had confidence in me, and they came to me with the request that I should draw up petitions for them. Whereas, if they used their common-sense, they would have realised that I must be bad-luck. They would have realised that if I was any good at drawing up petitions I would long ago have drawn up a petition for myself, successfully, with the result that I would no longer be in prison. The fact that I had done so many years of my stretch, without having got any time off on a petition, should have convinced my fellow-convicts that I was no good at appealing to the higher authorities for clemency. How could he save others when himself he could not save?

But my fellow-prisoners just wouldn't look at it that way. The longer I stayed in prison, the more years of my sentence that I completed, the more convinced they were that I knew the ropes. So I obliged them. I believe that I wrote upwards of a hundred petitions. And the scroll-work on the outer covers of these documents got better and better. I am certain that, after a while, whenever a petition arrived at head-office, the clerks in charge could spot right away (without knowing my name or who I was) that it was a sample of my work: the ornate capitals, the superb flourishes, the elevated and archaic diction. And the queer thing is that the results I achieved for other convicts were, on the whole, not bad. On several occasions I succeeded in getting a man's sentence cut in half.

4

And then, one day, a petition of my own, sent in by myself on my own behalf, succeeded. Just like that. Take it or leave it, but what I am telling you is a fact. I had sent in a petition on my own behalf. I had spent many nights in getting the scrolls and flourishes right, and in making sure that the language was at once dignified and impressive – and obsolete. The jargon I made use of was a masterpiece. It sounded much more like Norman-French than Saxon English.

Anyway, the upshot of the whole thing was that my petition succeeded. As I have said before – just like that. The chief warder sent for me, and he told me that my sentence had been reduced, on instructions from head-office, by two years and a specified number of months . . .

I went back to my cage immediately. I got hold of a pencil and a piece of paper, I started calculating furiously. So much off for the Prince of Wales's visit; so much off as first offender's good conduct remission; so much mitigation under the Flag Bill; and so much right now as a result of my successful petition. Well, dash it all, if it didn't mean that, everything taken off, I had only another eight months to do!

I couldn't believe it at first, of course. I had to go over the same figures time and again. I spent the whole night in my cage, until the lights went out, calculating the dates and inscriptions on my ticket. I had hardly any time to crawl around my cage: I was so busy doing these calculations. But there it was, in black and white. I had only another eight months of my sentence to do. Tempus fugit. That was what had happened to me, during all those years and months in which I was doing time. What was the past pluperfect of fugo? Fugit? Fugavit? I didn't know, any more, my Latin and my brain having grown equally rusty within the prison walls. All I realised, then, was that time had, in verity, flown. Tempus fugit. If I had worked that back-of-the-dictionary Latin tag into my petition as well, I would probably have got three full years off my time, instead of a mere two years and certain odd months.

But, seated in my cell that night, I realised that time had in sooth flown. It had slipped away through my fingers. Eheu, fugaces. Time had trickled through my hands like sand. How wonderful! The best years of my life had fled from me, never to return. But how magnificent! It meant that they would have to let me go, now. Only another eight months – what was that to me – I who had done years without blinking – much? All that those years behind walls and bars had done to me was that I had now gone potty, and that I crawled about my cell-floor on hands and knees, when the warders weren't looking. But otherwise I was all right. And I gloried in the thought that the best years of my life were now spent, wasted in prison; because until such time as my youth was spent and wasted I would not be able to return to the world of free men.

5

My time was up, now, all but a few lousy months, which I could do on my head. To me, what had happened was incredible, a miracle. I had started off on a prison-stretch of inordinate length, and here through the way the years had passed, one by one, I found myself on the last lap. I was so near outside, with those few months only to go, that I believed I could smell the beginning of a new season; it seemed to me that the fragrance of a springtime world was seeping through into the inner prison, mingling with and overcoming the stink of fear and ordure with which the whole prison was impregnated, always. I spoke to some of the other convicts about it, to some of the old lags who done lots of time, and for whom that moment of being discharged through the front gate of the prison held out no particular novelty.

And they said, yes, that was the marvel of doing time; the longest stretch came to an end, they said; and when you found yourself on the last lap, like I was now, it was difficult to believe that those years actually had been served, one by one, in the prison. You didn't know what had happened to those years, they said. It was only when you got back into the world outside that you realised that the years had indeed gone . . .

6

There was so much to be done, all at once. I had to arrange about having a suit made, for one thing. A real suit. Every convict who served more than two years was entitled to have a real suit, cut to his own measurements, made for him in the prison tailors' shop: and at a cost of only two pounds fourteen, to be paid for out of his gratuity. The price charged for the suit covered only the actual cost of the material, blue Government serge that had first-rate wearing qualities. All the labour that went into the making of the suit was given by the prison authorities free of charge.

It was wonderful, when a warder escorted me into the tailors' shop, and they took my measurements, and the head-warder in charge of the tailors' shop told me that I could choose any kind of style at all. So I chose a double-breasted suit; I said I wanted a twenty-four inch leg, at the bottom, and thirty-three inches long, and the jacket had to be short, the back of it coming just level with the bottom of my spine; and I wanted a rolled lapel, and the breast-pocket must be high up, please; and I gave them all sorts of other instructions like that; and the head-warder took it all down in pencil; and he said I could have my discharge suit just like I wanted it, and he always saw to it that the tailors' shop turned out the best work it knew how in making a first-class discharge suit for a long-timer going out.

And then I asked could I also have the shoulders padded straight and narrow, and the back draped. And it was then that the trades-warder took me aside and spoke to me very confidentially, and because of the earnest manner in which he spoke to me – and not because I really thought he was right – I allowed him to have his own way about the details of the cut.

"It's like this," the warder said to me, "You've been inside a good number of years, now, haven't you?"

"Yes," I answered – and I felt a deep satisfaction at the thought of the exact number.

"And during these years you have never worn a civilian suit?" the head-warder asked, "And you haven't seen a civilian suit, have you? You have seen only convicts in convict garb, and warders in warders' uniforms, haven't you?"

"That is so," I admitted.

"Well," he explained, "men's fashions have changed since you was last outside. They haven't changed much, mind you, but enough to make a bit of difference. And if I turn out a suit to your requirements, like you have specified now, well, it will be a very out-of-date suit that you'll walk on to the pavement with."

And so, reluctantly, I told him he could have his way about the cut. But I said what I really wanted was, when I walked, to to be able to feel my trouser-legs flapping about my shoes: flap, flap, I said. And he said, of course, that I could have.

And I went there often to be fitted. And they made a beautiful job of my Government serge suit, nearly all of it hand-sewn. And night after night I dreamt about that suit, and how lovely it was. And I spent most of my waking hours thinking how marvellous it would be to have a real suit, that I could hang in a wardrobe, or fold over a chair, or wear in the street. And there would be no numbers on the jacket or the trousers.

I did not know that, in actual reality, I would never again in my life wear a suit that did not have numbers on it.

I did not know, then, how a man who has once been in prison feels for the rest of his life when he is outside. For I left prison twenty years ago. And I have been conscious for every moment of the time, since then, that I am an ex-convict. Every suit I wear has got prison numbers plastered on it. If the world can't see those numbers, I can ... But the world can also see them, all right ... But this was something that I didn't know then, when I was having my blue serge suit fitted on me in the prison tailors' shop. I was romantically in love with that suit. It was only when I got into the outside world that I discovered that I would always have numbers on my jacket and a broad-arrow on the seat of my pants.

7

Those last eight months passed quickly. As a matter of fact, it turned out that it was a bit more than eight months. The clerk at head office in charge of my files had omitted to make certain calculations in respect of remission, with the result that, for some time, I was in the queer position of being a forgotten man. I have difficulty, even to-day, in explaining what that means. The day I was due for discharge I said to my section-warder, in the morning, "I am going out to-day," and I added, "I suppose I stay in the section until they send for the discharges, sir?"

The section-officer said, no, he hadn't been notified. But he knew I was going out, of course, quite soon. I had it on my ticket. And he knew that I had been measured for a suit. Anyway, I showed the section-warder my ticket, and we got a pencil and a piece of paper and we worked it out together.

There was no doubt about it. I was due for discharge, and right away.

"Anyway, I got no instructions," the section-warder said. "Fall in for work."

And in the workshop I showed my ticket to the head-warder, and he also worked out the figures, and he scratched his head, and looked puzzled. "But I can't do nothing about it," he assured me. "That's for the discipline staff. I am only a head trades-warder. So get on with your blooming job."

And I showed my ticket to a whole lot of convicts, and they worked it out, also, not with paper and pencil, because they didn't need to. A convict who had done lots of stretches only had to take a single glance at my ticket and through some sort of sixth sense, because he had done so much time, he could see at once that I was due for discharge.

"They must a lorst your papers at head-office," one blue-coat suggested. "That means you'll never get out. You don't exist for them, no more. I remember the case of —"

But I moved away quickly. I didn't want to hear any bad-luck stories. I was scared of ill-omened precedents.

Next day I saw the chief-warder in the office about my getting discharged. He also agreed with me that, as far as the law was concerned, I was a free man. It said so on my ticket.

"Yes," I acknowledged, "I am free. I am a free man. There's nothing to keep me here in prison any more. Nothing except the bars and the locks and the warders."

Anyway, the chief-warder informed me that it was no concern of his. All these things were done from head-office. All he could do was, when a discharge-warrant came from head-office for a convict, to order that convict's release. And he hadn't got such a discharge warrant from head-office for me. "But don't you worry," he assured me. "The moment that paper comes along, I'll see you get out. *I* won't keep you here a minute longer than I got to."

I thanked him very much. But was there nothing he could do about it?

"It seems to me like the clerk in charge of your file has sort of overlooked it," the chief-warder said. "Or he may be on leave. Or he may have forgotten to enter some of your remission – over the Flag Bill, perhaps. Or he may have lost your papers. I remember a case —"

But I asked the chief-warder please not to continue. I was afraid I might panic. If nothing was heard during the course of the next few days, might he perhaps take it up with the head office? He assured me that he would. "If you don't hear any more about it," he said, "Come and see me again in about a month's time."

I went to see him again, of course. And in much less than a month's time.

"But see, sir," I said, "I am here, am I not? And according to the details of my sentence and remission I have no right to be here. In theory I am not a hard-labour convict at all."

"What do you want, then?" the chief-warder enquired, in a nasty tone, "Do you want a job here as chief-warder, perhaps? Don't be afraid to ask, now."

But I informed him, trying hard to keep sane, that I didn't want any sort of job in the prison, and that I wanted no part of the prison, and that my one desire was to get as far away as possible from any contact with and any thought of the prison.

"It's your file at head-office," the chief-warder explained "Yes, something must have happened about your file. I'll go and see about it next chance I get of slipping away from the prison for an hour or so."

215

"Might that be to-day, sir, perhaps?" I enquired hopefully.

"Some time next month," the chief-warder answered, "Look, you've done a good long stretch, already, and we haven't had much trouble from you. I hope you aren't going to start being a nuisance now. What's a few extra months, anyway, on top of the time you have already done with a clean sheet? Just go back to the section, and enjoy yourself here a little longer, and it will all get fixed up."

I passed through a period of the most utter desolation. I felt so completely helpless and frustrated. And there was nothing I could do about it. I still get nightmares about that period. Here was I, in the prison, a human being, of flesh and air and bone; I existed here, in the prison, as a physical reality. At least, that was what I had always believed. But I found that I wasn't that person at all. I wasn't me. I wasn't this individual sitting here on a stool eating mealie-porridge out of a tin basin. Oh, no. This person did not exist at all, as an entity. It wasn't me, the person that had got his suit made – the suit that was all pressed and hung on a clothes-hanger in the tailors' shop, waiting for me to come and fetch it away. No, I wasn't this person at all.

What was really me were a lot of papers, dog-eared and yellowed with the years, lying between two cardboard covers and tied up with green string, in a filing cabinet at head-office ... I saw, now, why I had got claustrophobia, in prison. It wasn't because of the prison. Quite enough air came into my cage through the barred window. But that person in the steel cage wasn't me at all. My real individuality, my real *me*, were those papers in that filing-cabinet. So, of course, I had suffocation fears. Who wouldn't get claustrophobia, shut like that between two covers, and tied up with green string, and then locked into a steel cabinet – with more and more folders getting piled on top of me with each year that passed? How on earth can you breathe inside a steel cabinet?

But I don't want to go on piling up the horrors. It is enough to say that, shortly afterwards, through the friendly offices of the chief-warder, a vast stack of other folders were lifted from me, and I was taken out of the steel cabinet, and my covers were dusted, and the green string was untied . . .

8

As a result of this bit of confusion, I didn't get discharged from the prison, like other convicts, at nine o'clock in the morning. The warrant for my release arrived late one afternoon. It was marked urgent, in very large, black letters and it said that I was to be released immediately.

So they had to fetch a clerk from his home (because he had already gone off duty) to work out how much was due to me in gratuity and to make out an official cheque for me. Another warder escorted me to the stores, where they fitted me out with a pair of prison-made discharge boots. They went and dug up my suit-case, containing a couple of shirts that I had worn many years ago, before I was convicted. I put on a shirt with stripes. The cool, luxurious feel of light linen against my skin after all those years in which I had worn the coarse, stinking, degrading – oh, never mind: the sensation of linen lying lightly on my body was exquisite. There was also a tie in my suit-case, a bright piece of neckwear that had not faded, very appreciably, during the length of time in which it had been thrust away from the world, in a dark corner. They had not put me in prison, alone, but my few poor possessions also. I didn't realise, until now, that I had had my suitcase and my socks and my shirts to keep me company during the period of my incarceration. I picked up that tie with a warm feeling of intimacy. My friendly old tie; my companion in imprisonment; here we were meeting again; and he was still gaudy; he still had memories of former gaieties, brightly-dyed; he was still half-cheeky. I wondered whether I was like my tie in this respect; whether I also, at the end of my imprisonment, retained something inside me that was bright-hued. But I feared not. My tie didn't have to say "Yes, sir," all day long.

And then, of course, when I had it round my neck, I didn't know how to fasten that tie. Through all that long disuse my fingers had lost the trick of knotting a tie around my neck. A warder performed the office for me.

And then I found that I couldn't get my suit. It was locked up in the tailors' shop. They couldn't get the key. It was a blow But they fitted me out with an ordinary prison discharge suit, called a pom-pom, which the Government supplies to short-timer discharged convicts. It didn't look very elegant, but they said it would do for the night. Next morning I could call round at the prison, at the front-gate, and my blue serge suit would be neatly parcelled-up there for me.

"Please see to it that they don't crush my suit when they fold it," I said to a discipline warder. But I hadn't much faith that they would exercise the right amount of care.

The final formalities were gone through. I was given my discharge papers. It was explained to me that mine was a conditional release. I was being let out on ticket-of-leave. The conditions of my discharge were read out to me: they were contained in two pages of print. Then I shook hands with the warders about me and I took up my suit-case and my prison-discharge boots sounded clumsy on the cement-floor of the court-yard before the main-gate. And the gate swung open. Not very much. Just enough to let me out.

And I was free.

The guard at the gate shook hands with me. And he called me by my name instead of by my number.

"Look after yourself, now," the gate-warder said, "You know boob is a bastard. See you don't come back."

I answered, "Yes, thank you, sir."

Forgetting that I no longer had any need to call him "sir".

Epilogue

This is really a love story – a story of adolescent love, my first love . . . Her eyes were heavily fringed with dark lashes, like barred windows. Her bosom was hard and pure and cold – like a cement floor. And it was a faithful and chaste love. During all those years of my young manhood, in whose arms did I sleep each night, but in hers?

2

And I feel a queer sort of spiritual intimacy with other men who have been in prison. Villon and Verlaine; and Oscar Wilde and O. Henry and St. Paul.

And I feel that if one were to say to Francois Villon, "I think nothing of your poetry, man. That Great Testament of yours, now. And the Ballad of the Lords of Old Time. Second-rate stuff, man."

And Villon would answer, "Yes, that's all nothing. But I did time with One-Eyed Raoul."

Immediately you move up closer to Villon. "What!" you say, and there is incredulity in your voice, "Not One-Eyed Raoul. Surely not him? Did you really do time along with One-Eyed Raoul?"

"Yes," Villon would affirm proudly, "I was in prison the same time as him."

"And did you call him Raoul, like that, to his face?" you ask, "And did you also call him, familiarly, One-Eye? And did you grasp his hand in friendship?"

"No," Villon would answer, "You see, One-Eyed Raoul regarded me as a rat. He never spoke to me. He was a long-timer, One-Eyed Raoul."